THE
PREACHER'S
HANDBOOK

EDITED BY

DAVID N. FRANCIS

M.A.

NUMBER EIGHT

THE EPWORTH PRESS

FIRST PUBLISHED IN 1963

© THE EPWORTH PRESS 1963

Book Steward
FRANK H. CUMBERS

SET IN MONOTYPE PLANTIN AND PRINTED IN
GREAT BRITAIN BY HAZELL WATSON AND VINEY LTD
AYLESBURY AND SLOUGH

GENERAL PREFACE

The Preacher's Handbook (Number One) was published in July 1949 as an experiment and a venture of faith. We dared to believe that it might meet a real need among preachers. In particular, it was planned to serve and help the layman who may not feel he has the time or training to cope adequately with more profound and formidable books. He may be quite ready to equip himself, by study, to love God with all his mind; but he needs his material in more compact compass and more readily readable. We sought to meet this need.

We had in mind primarily the great body of 'local preachers' in the Methodist Church; but we hoped that those in other communions also, who are called to preach the Gospel, might find such a handbook equally helpful.

Our hopes were realized. It was soon evident that *The Preacher's Handbook* was meeting a real need. So much so that we have felt amply justified since in preparing and publishing a further *Handbook* every two years, the present issue being the eighth in this series. The earlier issues have been very widely read. Quite apart from private study, they are frequently used in preachers' fellowships and training-classes, as textbooks for corporate study and discussion.

These *Handbooks* are so planned that together they form a most valuable and compact library of material helpful to the preacher. New readers, of *Number Eight*, will doubtless feel drawn thereafter to secure and study also the earlier issues; and we would encourage them to do so, where they are still available. (We regret that *Nos. One* to *Three* are now out of print.)

NOTE—*The Preacher's Handbooks* are planned and sponsored by the Local Preachers' Department of the Methodist Church, 1 Central Buildings, Westminster, S.W.1; and are published by the Epworth Press, 25–35 City Road, London, E.C.1.

EDITORIAL

QUITE clearly *The Preacher's Handbook* has come to stay. Seven, we know, is a good biblical number, and there was a time—years ago—when we wondered whether Number Seven might not well complete the series. But very evidently that would have been a mistake. The interest in *The Preacher's Handbook* continues unabated; each new issue is awaited with eagerness, and there are many enthusiasts who have carefully collected the whole series.

Such preachers are wise, of course; not only because of the proved value of each new issue, but because these volumes are planned to link up with one another. Together, as a series, they tend to become an increasingly useful reference library for the wise collector. Unfortunately, the newcomer in this field will no longer be able to collect any of the first four of the eight issues—unless he is quick to secure one of the few remaining copies of *Number Four*.

We believe that *Number Eight* will be found to maintain very worthily the high standard set by its predecessors. Once again there is indeed treasure here, for those who have a mind to seek diligently. And once again the 'fare' that we have sought to set before you is very varied indeed—something to suit all reasonable tastes, and as a whole a very balanced diet! We are much indebted, as hitherto, to our various contributors; and to our publishers, the Epworth Press, for their constant co-operation.

It will be noted that two of the articles in this *Handbook* are from contributors who—in one sense only—are no longer with us. Alex Findlay died shortly after he had specially written for us his 'Glimpses of the Life of Jesus', the second part of which now appears in this volume. And Alan Kay was revising and preparing his material for us, on 'The Preacher's Use of Words', at the time of his death. We salute two quite outstanding men of God; and we shall remain deeply indebted to them both.

*　　　*　　　*

Two years ago, when editing *Number Seven*, I expanded this Editorial slightly, to include not only a word about this series and the new addition to it, but also some thoughts of a more general character concerning the place of the lay or 'local' preacher in the Church, and his changing and growing responsibilities. This 'thinking aloud' was apparently a help to some; much correspondence ensued, and evidently many were stimulated to fresh thinking. So it is that, emboldened by this experience, I am now daring to carry this discussion a stage further.

In our own Methodist Church—I hope other readers will forgive this domestic excursion—the local preacher occupies a special and unique position. We have got used to his presence, and we take for granted his quite invaluable contribution to the life and work of our Church. We are now only vaguely aware that three out of four of our services are conducted by local preachers, and can hardly believe that without them Methodism would grind to a standstill tomorrow. Yet it would; for the whole complex machinery of this highly organized Church of ours is built firmly upon the assumption that we have—and can depend upon—this particular lay ministry.

It *is* a *particular* lay ministry, too. I sometimes wonder if we all realize just how particular, how really unique in Methodism this lay ministry is. We have many kinds of lay workers in our Church—interpreting 'lay' for this purpose as those who are not 'full-time' and not ordained—and we owe much to them all. But the local preacher is the only lay worker in Methodism who is tested and trained connexionally: that is, by the Church as a whole. He is the only lay worker who, when trained, is recognized and authorized by the Church as a whole. He is the only lay worker who then receives a status that holds good throughout the Church as a whole. And he is the only lay worker drawn into a disciplined fellowship which extends throughout the Church as a whole. Thus in a fourfold sense he stands in a unique category; and this, not in his own right—no claim is made that as a person he is more good or more important than his brother—but because we believe that the call to conduct worship and to proclaim the Gospel stands in a category all on its own. When this call comes, it marks and claims a man; here, in this call, is something we dare not ignore, must not smother, and should never simply equate with 'other forms of Christian service'.

This is a vital part of the genius of Methodism. Even though it came to us through improvisation and experimentation, we can now see that God was in this unique development. And in this concept today, in this distinctive lay ministry, we have a big and important contribution to make to 'the Coming Great Church'.

I am sometimes asked—somewhat apprehensively—'What place will there be for the lay preacher if Methodism unites with other communions?' I am quite sure that he will be more needed, not less. It is significant that the Anglicans, with whom now we have been having exploratory 'Conversations', are recognizing increasingly the importance of the laity, and giving far more attention than hitherto to the lay reader—his recruitment and training, his place in the life of the Church and his responsibilities. In any 'Coming Great Church', the Methodist Church will have much to offer along this line, out of its unique experience with lay preachers.

Provided always—! Yes, there are indeed prerequisites, conditions that Methodism will need to observe, if this contribution is to be a real and valuable one.

Some of these conditions must be met by the local preacher himself. One, very clearly, is this: he must look to his standards, the *quality* of what he is, and does, and offers in his distinctive form of Christian service. Mediocrity just will not do, particularly today.

In this connection it is significant and cheering to note how many preachers are recognizing the need to equip themselves more adequately. There were never so many 'tools for the job' as there are available today; and they are being used. There were never so many training classes, schools, and conferences planned specially for preachers; and they are well supported.

Particularly noteworthy is the growing recognition that lay preachers need systematic training, not only in biblical and doctrinal subjects but in the practical work of leading in worship, and of preaching the Gospel. Hence the new and serious consideration that the Methodist Church is now giving to the desirability of making 'Worship and Preaching' an essential subject in the training of local preachers, and not just an optional 'extra', as hitherto.

Another essential condition, if the local preacher is to fulfil his rôle worthily in the Church of tomorrow, is this: he must be *versatile*. It is not enough that he should be prepared to take services, as appointed on the Circuit Plan. He must be adaptable to changing circumstances, ready to witness in other ways, willing to find new contacts. He must not be bound by the assumption that his only sphere of service is a Methodist pulpit, and that Sunday (11 or 6.30) brings him his only opportunity to share the good news. He must no longer assume that it is the duty of his Church to provide him with a ready-made congregation.

When God called us, it was not just to become a particular kind of preacher in a particular Church. He called us to listen for His word and then to proclaim it, to share the good news about Him, to love and care for people, and to seek to bring them to Him. Our commission is as wide as that, and 'the taking of services' is only part of it. Not only the needs of the modern world, but our own knowledge of God and of His yearning compel us to be ever seeking for fresh ways of serving Him, ever ready for new and less conventional opportunities for witness.

These may be within the life of the local Christian community —and woe be to the preacher who has not got his roots deep down in the life of a particular church! Or they may be in the preacher's neighbourhood—the beginning of a new house-fellowship, for instance, centred in his own home. Or they may be found within the setting of his daily work, or his trade or civic contacts. The lay preacher who is ready for adventures has many openings as a 'worker-priest'; and in these days, with institutional Christianity at a discount, it is the more necessary for him to seek them. If the world will not come to the Church, then the Church must go to the world.

Quality and *Versatility*: these are undoubtedly 'musts' for modern preachers. But there are other 'musts' which apply to their congregations, and to the Church that has confirmed their call. Again we mention two.

One is the urgent need for Christian people to do some new thinking about *the place and significance of the lay preacher in the life of the Church.* Is he just a reserve, a temporary 'stop-gap' in case of need? Or do we really believe in a lay ministry as a deliberate and significant part of God's plan? And if so, is the whole community of God's people giving sufficient attention to the training of its lay preachers, and to a right use of them when trained? And again, is the Church seeking to understand and loyally to support the lay preachers whom it has recognized, and to exalt the Order to which they belong?

The other major responsibility of the Church in this connection is surely *in the realm of recruitment.* We need to teach the fact of divine vocation: that when God calls anyone He also assigns tasks for him to take up. Every Christian disciple is called for service, and needs to discover what his allotted task is: 'What shall I *do*, Lord?'

There must be many people within the Christian Church

whom God is calling for this particular work, the proclaiming of His Gospel and the winning of others. We need to discover—with infinite wisdom and respect for human personality—who they are. And then we must help them to understand what this call means, and to respond aright.

Nor must we only look for 'those whom God may be calling' when *we* need them, when the *local* situation cries out for more preachers. We must recognize that God sees further than we can, and sometimes calls even when there seems to be no immediate and local need. We must not be just parochial, governed only by expediency. If this be God's authentic summons then we *must recognize and honour it*, and give it expression within the life of the local church. This may sometimes be difficult, but it can be done. And one day—if this call was indeed of God—we shall see how important it was that it should be done.

DAVID N. FRANCIS

CONTENTS

PART ONE

General Articles

1. The Local Preacher in Early Methodism

By the REV. JOHN C. BOWMER, M.A., B.D.

IN *The Proceedings of the Wesley Historical Society* the late Mr Duncan Coomer once wrote, 'Among the institutions of early Methodism, that of local preachers is the one whose record is the haziest.[1] That is a statement of fact which further studies amply confirm. John Wesley was a great organizer, and in the course of his providing for the well-being of the people called Methodists, he laid down rules for all sorts and conditions of men —for Itinerant Preachers, Helpers, Stewards, Society and Band Members, for the Preachers' Fund and for Congregational singing. But in all this effort to regulate the life of early Methodism, nothing is laid down for local preachers. The Journals and the Letters of the Wesley brothers, the Minutes of the early Conferences supply sporadic references to local preachers, but nowhere are they fully integrated into the organization of Methodism.[2] Our first duty must be to seek an explanation of this, so far as the available references will enable us to do so.

The Local Preacher of today has a double ancestry. On the one hand, there were those who were known simply as 'The Preachers'. At first they were full-time, but not ordained. Their distinguishing title was, 'Itinerant Preachers'. Subsequently, they constituted the Methodist Ministry. However, be they Itinerant

[1] Vol. xxv, p. 33.
[2] For reasons which will become apparent as we proceed, it will be advisable to print the term 'local preacher' without capitals, thus indicating that during this period it was not a technical term. There was no Order or organization which gave a person the status of a 'Local Preacher' in the modern sense of the term. A 'local preacher' in early Methodism simply meant a layman who preached locally, as distinct from an itinerant preacher who was 'full time' in the work.

Preachers or Methodist Ministers, they all began their career as local preachers.

At the same time, there was another class of men, ancestors of our present-day Local Preachers; they were known as 'Exhorters'. In the early days, when the itinerants became a recognized body of men in the connexion, these exhorters were the nearest in function to what we know as Local Preachers today. Their main characteristic was that they operated locally, leading prayer meetings and addressing societies and classes.[3] Let us therefore turn, first to 'preachers' and then to exhorters in early Methodism.

METHODIST PREACHERS

We must begin with a consideration of those who were simply styled 'Methodist Preachers'—men like John Cennick, Thomas Maxfield and Joseph Humphreys.[4] Nor must we forget that noble band of men whose stirring religious experience is written in the six volumes, *Lives of the Early Methodist Preachers*.[5] These men were not local preachers in the later sense of the term, but they were lay preachers as distinct from Wesley and the clergy. They fitted into the Methodist pattern something like this. The society met in its own 'room', generally under the leadership of Class Leaders who also provided pastoral oversight, but worship in its wider aspects was supplied by the parish church. Circuit Plans were a thing of the future, and the devotional needs of the societies were met by the itinerants and the Class Leaders. If, as occasionally happened, some individual in the society displayed a gift for preaching and desired to exercise it further, he was given an opportunity of joining the ranks of the Itinerant Preachers. From a reference in the Minutes of 1763 it is evident that the Itinerants were recruited from the ranks of the local preachers and that every opportunity was given for able preachers to become itinerants:

In several parts of England there are local preachers who have both gifts and graces equal to those of most itinerants. Why then do they not travel?[6]

[3] See Jackson, *Life of Charles Wesley*, i, 444.
[4] See additional note, 'Who was the first Methodist Local Preacher?'
[5] Or in seven volumes, *Wesley's Veterans*. On the relationship between *Lives of the E.M.P.* and *Wesley's Veterans*, see *Proceedings of the W.H.S.*, xxii, 102.
[6] Minutes (1862 edition), vol. i, p. 626.

Before a local preacher became an itinerant, however, he had to submit to an oral examination before Wesley and his colleagues. As early as 1746, a question was asked in the Conference, 'How shall we try those who believe they are moved by the Holy Ghost and called of God to preach?' The answer given is:

Inquire, 1. Do they know in whom they have believed? 2. Have they gifts (as well as grace) for the work? 3. Have they success? We will send one of our Helpers to hear him preach . . . and . . . we will desire him to relate or to write down the reasons which he believes he is called of God to preach.[7]

One cannot forbear to quote Dr Leslie Church's comment on these words:

It is a far cry from these decisions of the Conference in 1746 to the institution of theological colleges or to highly specialized courses of study for local preachers, but the vital tests are still the same. Grace—gifts—fruits! These have been the fundamental qualifications of Methodist preachers, ministerial or lay, for more than two centuries.[8]

So we begin with these men in the early Methodist societies who felt the call to preach and who, if they sought further and regular means of service, were encouraged, indeed expected to join the ranks of the itinerant preachers. The relationship between these local prachers and the Itinerants has been well expressed by Dr Leslie Church:

To be able to endure the hardships of a travelling preacher's life demanded absolute physical fitness, freedom from business ties, and, as far as possible, from domestic responsibilities. Many of those who could not meet all these conditions became 'local' preachers, but this did not necessarily imply that they were less capable than their brethren, who went farther afield. Generally speaking, their reading was more limited and they did not, of course, enjoy such close contact with John Wesley, nor the benefits of his supervision. The Bible, Milton's *Paradise Lost* or Young's *Night Thoughts*, the Methodist Hymn Book, and perhaps a stray volume of the *Arminian Magazine* or the 'Christian Library', would embrace the main portion of their 'literary apparatus'.[9]

Further light on these preachers and their place in the societies must now be sought from the writings of Wesley.

The first reference to local preachers in Wesley's Journal appears to be under the date of 31st December, 1777, when 'four

---

[7] Minutes, i, 30–31.
[8] Church, L. F.: *More about the Early Methodist People*, p. 102.
[9] Ibid., p. 104.

or five of the local preachers' assisted him at the London Watch-
night Service. He comments:

I was agreeably surprised, their manner of praying being so artless and
unlaboured, and yet rational and scriptural, both as to sense and expression.

Then on 6th February, 1789, 'being the quarterly day for meeting the local preachers', Wesley says that between twenty and
thirty of the local preachers met at West Street Chapel. This is
one of those tantalizing entries in the Journal which gives just
enough information to whet the appetite for more. The question
we naturally ask is, 'Is this meeting, apparently one of a series held
quarterly, to be regarded as the predecessor of our Quarterly
Local Preachers Meeting?' Apart from the single reference, we
do not know when Quarterly Circuit Local Preachers Meetings
were first begun, what their nature was, or if they were held
consistently and where. Unfortunately, there is no reference to
them in any rules and regulations of early Methodism before 1796,
nor do they appear to be really widespread until the beginning of
the nineteenth century.

At the Conference of 1796 the question was asked, 'How shall
we prevent improper persons from insinuating into the Society?';
and part of the reply read:

Respecting the admission of persons to be Local Preachers, let the
Assistant regularly meet the Local Preachers once a quarter, and let
none be admitted but those that are proposed and approved at that
Meeting; and, if in any Circuit this be not practicable, let them be proposed and approved at the Quarterly Meeting.[10]

The feeling, expressed above, that Quarterly Local Preachers
Meetings did not become widespread until well into the nineteenth century is strengthened by the fact that in a series of plans
of the Leeds Circuit beginning at 1777, the first mention of a
Local Preachers Meeting comes in 1810.

A reference to local preachers in Wesley's Journal for 8th June,
1781, shows the system developing as we know it today. Speaking
of the Isle of Man, Wesley says:

The local preachers are men of faith and love, knit together in one mind
and one judgement. They speak either Manx or English, and follow a
regular plan which the assistant gives them monthly.

This does not imply that a printed 'Local Preachers' Plan' was
published. It was probably a hand-written list of appointments

[10] Minutes, i, 366.

circulated among the local preachers. As a matter of fact, the earliest plan in existence is that referred to above for the Leeds Circuit, dated 1777. The circuit of forty-four societies (excluding the town chapel) is divided into two halves—one half having a preaching service one Sunday and the other half on the next Sunday, and so on. As this plan consists of local preachers only, it would appear that a separate plan was issued for the itinerant preachers.[11]

Turning from the Journal to the Letters of John Wesley, such references to local preachers as are to be found there are largely (and unfortunately) concerned with discipline. In a letter to George Whitefield in 1767, Wesley makes a clear distinction between the 'travelling' and the 'local' preacher:

We are so far from having any travelling preacher to spare that there are not enough to supply people that earnestly call for them—but some of the local preachers are equal both in grace and gifts to most of the itinerants.[12]

This reference to local preachers ante-dates the first Journal reference by ten years, so at least we can say that Wesley was acknowledging the usefulness and gifts of local preachers as early as 1767.

The argument from silence is notoriously precarious, but the absence of any reference to local preachers in a letter written to Vincent Perronet in 1748 indicates that local preachers did not constitute part of the set-up of Methodism at that time. Wesley says:

It remains only to give you a short account of those who serve their brethren in love. There are the Leaders of the Classes and Bands. . . . Assistants, Stewards, Visitors of the Sick and Schoolmasters. . . .[13]

From the Journal and Letters of Wesley, we turn to the Minutes of Conference. From the Minutes it would seem that local preachers, as distinct from 'travelling' preachers, emerged soon after the letter to Vincent Perronet just quoted, that is during the decade 1750–60, though it is clear that the title 'local preacher' is not always used. Sometimes we read of 'preachers in one place' and in one instance (and only one, so far as we know) of 'half itinerants'.

Lists of those who attended the early Conferences are not without interest for our study. There is no evidence that local preachers attended the first Conference in 1744, but three years

[11] Reproduced in Smith, G.: *History of Wesleyan Methodism*, i, 702.
[12] Letters, v, 44–45.   [13] Letters, ii, 304.

later we are told that there were present 22 preachers (that is, itinerants) and 38 who 'assisted chiefly in one place'.[14] Among the latter we notice the names of Christopher Hopper and William Shent. We know that Shent never resigned his barber's shop in Leeds, but left it in the charge of an apprentice while he went off on his preaching tours. In fact, in 1755 he is quite appropriately described as a 'half itinerant'.

At the Conference of 1753, there were present 28 'travelling preachers' and 12 'local preachers'.[15] The Minutes for 1755 speak of 'our present itinerant preachers' and 'our chief local preachers'.[16] There is also a list of 12 'half itinerants' among whom, as we remarked above, is William Shent. This is the first and only time this term is used. It never becomes an official term in Methodism, but in its day it evidently denoted a person who fulfilled a duty somewhere between the full-time itinerant and the local preacher. It is impossible to be more precise.

After 1755 references to local preachers in the Minutes are only sporadic, a fact which is all the more disappointing when it is remembered that this was the period during which the forms and traditions of Methodism were taking shape. In 1789 Wesley appeared to be meeting the local preachers quarterly and Quarterly Meetings for Local Preachers are referred to in the Minutes of 1796. Dr Beecham, writing on the Constitution of Methodism in 1851, expressed the following opinion:

Up to the year 1771 we have no mention of local preachers meetings. Some time previous to the death of Wesley, the assistants had met the local preachers occasionally, more especially when the new circuit plans were about to be made, but from the great extent of many of the circuits, this could not be a universal practice. It was not till the year 1796, five years after Mr Wesley's death, that any formal recognition was made of local preachers meetings. Then it was enacted that from time to time, wherever it could be found practicable, the superintendent should meet the local preachers every quarter and that instead of its being left entirely to the assistant to take on the plan whomsoever he saw fit, none should thenceforth be admitted but those who were approved of at that meeting or at the quarterly meetings of the circuit where local preachers meetings could not be held.[17]

This quotation confirms what is clear from other sources, that originally, and up to 1796, local preachers were not appointed by any official body in Methodism: rather their choice and appointment was entirely in the hands of the 'assistant', that is, the

[14] Minutes, i, 37. [15] Minutes i, 717.
[16] Minutes, i, 710–11. [17] p. 11.

superintendent. The rules of 1796 were obviously designed to bring local preachers into the orbit of official Methodism to whom, also, they would be accountable.

In 1832, the same Dr Beecham whom we have just quoted, received a letter from Dr Jabez Bunting, who wrote:

It will be well to ascertain from Mr James Wood, or some other aged preacher, whether Methodism, as Mr Wesley left it, knew nothing of Local Preachers' Meetings. The rule quoted by you may be the first statute in our code on the subject of such meetings, and yet, in point of fact, they might be previously held and so, from usage be part of our ancient common law.[18]

The rule referred to is that in the Minutes of 1796 which we have already referred to. One wishes that the words of 'some other aged preacher' had been recorded for our guidance on this point. It does seem certain, however, from this quotation that when Bunting was writing (1832) the origin of the first Local Preachers Meeting was not only unrecorded, but had also faded from memory. In fact, Pierce's *Ecclesiastical Principles and Polity of the Wesleyan Methodists* confesses to ignorance, not only of the first Quarterly Local Preachers Meeting, but of the origin of local preachers as a whole: 'We are unable to ascertain,' he says, 'the precise time when Mr Wesley first employed Lay Preachers in the Itinerancy.'[19] Dr W. B. Pope, writing in 1879, says:

When the name Local Preacher was first invented no man knows; certainly, I do not.[20]

The Conference rules of 1796 have already been quoted in so far as they refer to Quarterly Local Preachers' Meetings; it might now be opportune to quote them in full. They constitute the first tangible guidance we possess in our search for origins in Local Preachers' affairs. The question asked was, 'What can be done to bring certain Local Preachers more fully to observe our discipline?' Actually, the point was raised on a question of discipline, and the answers given were as follows:

1. Let no one be permitted to preach who will not meet in class, and who is not regularly planned by the Superintendent of the Circuit where he resides.

2. Let no Local Preacher be allowed to preach in any other Circuit where he lives; or suffer any invitation to be admitted as a plea, whether

---

[18] Bunting, T. P.: *Life of Jabez Bunting*, ii, p. 256.   [19] p. 9.
[20] Pamphlet in the Library of the Wesley Historical Society, 'The Methodist Local Preacher,' p. 23.

from men in office or not, without the previous knowledge and full consent of the Superintendent of the place where any one may ask him to
preach.

3. Let no Local Preacher keep love-feasts without the appointment of
the Superintendent, nor in any way interfere with his business, as mentioned in the Large Minutes. We must carefully attend to our rules, that
all things may be done decently and in order.[21]

Joseph Entwisle, writing in 1783, gives a valuable picture of
what happened before there were any rules and regulations for
Local Preachers:

My name was placed on the circuit plan and I continued to labour as
a local preacher above four years. There were no printed plans in those
days. The superintendent of the circuit or the assistant as he was then
called, when he had prepared the draught [sic] used to employ a person
to write out a copy, in a fair and legible hand, for each of the local
preachers.[22]

So much, then for the local preachers, their origins and their
duties. We must now turn our attention to that other class of
preachers known as 'Exhorters'.

EXHORTERS

The earliest reference to Exhorters seems to be found in
Charles Wesley's Journal. He says that on 30th June, 1746, he
met some Exhorters at Gwennap in Cornwall. As a result of much
persecution the Methodists had been scattered, but, to use
Charles Wesley's own words:

the Lord gathered them again, and kept them together by their own
brethren; who began to exhort their companions, one or more in every
society. No less than four have sprung up in Gwennap. . . . I advised
and charged them not to stretch themselves beyond their line, by speaking out of the Society, or fancying themselves public teachers. . . .

He talked to another Exhorter on 13th July and on the 21st at St
Just he met, 'their exhorter' who, he says, 'appeared a solid,
humble Christian, raised up to stand in the gap, and keep the
trembling sheep together'.

The following year, John Wesley met these Cornish Exhorters
and the reference to them in his Journal is worth quoting in full:

[21] Minutes, i, 361.
[22] Smith, G.: *History of Wesleyan Methodism*, i, 640, quoting *Memoirs
of the Rev. Joseph Entwisle*, p. 15.

On Thursday (June 9th, 1747) the stewards of all the societies met. I now diligently inquired what exhorters there were in each society; whether they had gifts meet for the work; whether their lives were eminently holy; and whether there appeared any fruit of their labour. I found, upon the whole: (1) That there were no less than eighteen exhorters in the county. (2) That three of these had no gifts at all for the work, neither natural nor supernatural. (3) That a fourth had neither gifts nor grace; but was a dull, empty, self-conceited man. (4) That a fifth had considerable gifts, but had evidently made shipwreck of the grace of God. These, therefore, I determined immediately to set aside, and advise our societies not to hear them. (5) That J.B., A.L., and J.W., had gifts and grace, and had been much blessed in the work. Lastly, that the rest might be helpful when there was no preacher in their own or the neighbouring societies, provided they would take no step without the advice of those who had more experience than themselves.

According to a letter written by John Bennet, in which he refers to what may have been the first Circuit Quarterly Meeting, he says that 'several exhorters were present'.[23] However, apart from this isolated reference no more is said about these Exhorters, their character or their function. At the same time, it is among the Exhorters that we get the first signs of any attempt to organize this class of workers in early Methodism. In the Minutes of the 1746 Conference, the following direction was given:

Let none exhort in any of our Societies without a note of recommendation from the assistant. Let every exhorter see that this is renewed yearly. Let every assistant rigorously insist upon this.[24]

The Conference of 1770 asked, 'How shall each Assistant know the Exhorters in his circuit?' The answer was:

Let each give his successor a list of them.[25]

Here we may detect the origin of the Circuit Plan.

It could therefore be said that in those early days, the Exhorters were the nearest we have to our modern Local Preachers, except that they operated only in their own society.[26]

[23] This was at Todmorden Edge. See Simon, J. S.: *John Wesley and the Advance of Methodism*, p. 157.

[24] Minutes, i, 570.

[25] Minutes, i, 94.

[26] It is of interest to note that the term 'Exhorter' is still used in some circuits for men and women who do not reach the status of a fully qualified Local Preacher, but who are able to give limited—yet effective—service in the pulpit. The term is not, however, officially recognized or encouraged. The growing tendency is for all preachers to be drawn into the full fellowship and discipline of the Circuit Local Preachers Meeting.

CONCLUSIONS

Having examined the situation during the lifetime of John Wesley and having noted most of the references, we can now proceed to draw our conclusions.

The most significant question which is raised by our study is, 'Why has Wesley so little to say about local preachers, especially during the last two decades of his life when evidently their services were becoming increasingly necessary and when so much of our permanent organization was being fashioned?'

In the first place, Methodism was developing from a federation of societies into a Church with an obligation to its people to provide a satisfying diet of worship and the sacraments. The 'Churchly' functions had to be assimilated into the organization of Methodism, with its well-knit economy with rules and regulations for all within its ranks (except the local preacher!); and when we remember the part which local preachers have played in the development of our Church, and the vital part they play today in the maintaining of its Sunday worship, we wonder that there is so little mention of them in the early days.

In the second place, we must remember that Wesley's conception of Methodism did not require the services of local preachers. He likened his organization to a well-regulated machine with each cog in its right place. Local Preachers, however, were not one of those cogs; in the Deed of Declaration of 1784 only Itinerants and ordained clergy of the Church of England were authorized to occupy the pulpits of Methodism. Local Preachers are not referred to at all.

One reason for this is not hard to find. Mr Coomer has rightly said, 'Methodism, in its essence, was the society *meeting*, not the Church *worshipping*.'[27] This is a valuable distinction which is not always kept in mind by students of Methodist origins. Many of the problems which have teased Methodism throughout its history, and still produce difficulties for our Connexional Committees today, lie in the unreconciled tensions between Methodism as a federation of societies and Methodism as a Church. In the early days of our connexion there was no need for local preachers. As a federation of societies it was not called upon to provide Christian worship in the full sense of that word. Methodist preaching presupposed the worship of the parish church[28] which

[27] *Proceedings W.H.S.*, xxv, 40. (Dr Coomer's italics.)
[28] Wesley's Works (3rd edition), viii, 321–2.

preachers and members alike were expected to attend. In this arrangement the Itinerant Preachers visited and directed the societies, the Class Leaders and Stewards took care of the spiritual and financial affairs—but for local preachers there was no place.

At the same time, it is clear that before Wesley died, Methodism was already becoming a Church *worshipping* as well as a society *meeting*; already there were pulpits to fill and preachers to find. Did Wesley not see this ? Or, if he did, why did he not acknowledge the need for local preachers and provide for them in the organization of the connexion, as his successors had to do within five years of his death ? The answer to these questions is not easy to find, but we might suggest three factors.

1. In the first place, either Wesley was not able or he did not choose to bring the local preachers directly under his personal supervision. Unlike the Itinerant Preachers, whom he always appointed himself, local preachers were chosen by the assistant.[29] At the same time, he did his best to keep a careful check on who was admitted and what was preached. An item of the Minutes of the 1752 Conference is enlightening here. The question asked was, 'Should any set up for a preacher in any place without the approbation of an assistant ?' The answer given is:

By no means. That has already been attended with ill consequences.[30]

This not only confirms that local preachers were under the Assistants' rather than Wesley's direct supervision, but also leads us to the second clue as to Wesley's hesitancy in making use of them.

2. In the second place, there was the question of discipline. At one time or another, preachers (apart from full-time Itinerants) had been a source of considerable trouble. Certain roving preachers had brought discredit upon early Methodism and generally speaking they were looked upon with suspicion by the civil authorities. Unfortunately, roving, freelance preachers were not uncommon in the eighteenth century. They were of doubtful origin and of even more doubtful doctrine and methods. Something of their reputation is hinted at by Wesley in a letter to Mary Bishop, dated 18th October, 1778:

Let but a pert, self-sufficient animal, that has neither sense nor grace, bawl out something about Christ and His blood or justification by faith, and his hearers cry out, 'What a fine gospel sermon!'[31]

---

[29] See above, p. 9.   [30] Minutes, i, 715.   [31] Letters, vi, 326.

Wesley had to be careful lest men of this reputation claimed the name of Methodist. In fact one of the charges which 'John Smith' (probably Thomas Secker, Bishop of Oxford) levied against Wesley was that he employed 'a number of unsent persons going about and preaching the worst of heresies'.[32] There was a constant danger that Wesley's preachers should be classed with these arrogant, undisciplined men. Perhaps it is to such that Wesley refers in his letter to James Barry on 24th June, 1776:

> . . . several of them (i.e. the local preachers) talk nonsense and some of them speak against perfection. This must not be suffered. Fix a regular plan for the local preachers and see that they keep it. You cannot be too exact in this and every part of discipline.[33]

In a letter to Samuel Bradburn dated 6th November, 1781, Wesley wrote:

> You must clip the wings of those local preachers who do not punctually observe your directions.[34]

and he repeated the same advice to Duncan Wright.[35] As early as 1747 he had been compelled to caution the Cornish societies against 'exhorters who had made shipwreck of the grace of God'[36] and in the next year had to warn his people against 'a cheat and impostor', Thomas Moor (alias Smith).[37] At Margate a freelance preacher had made havoc of a small Methodist society. 'Some years ago,' says Wesley in 1785, 'we had a small society here; but a local preacher took them to himself.'[38] Thus the second reason for the slow emergence of the local preacher on the Methodist scene is to be seen against the background of these undisciplined freelance preachers and Wesley's anxiety, in the absence of his personal supervision mentioned above, not to commit Methodism to what he could not himself fully control. We cannot but say that he was right, for it was this very point (i.e. bringing the local preachers under authoritative control and supervision) which led to the 1796 regulations.[39]

3. There is, however, a third reason for the tardy acknowledgement of local preachers in early Methodism, and that is to be found, regretfully, in Wesley's own personal reluctance to do so.

---

[32] Letters, ii, 98—July 1747.
[34] Letters, vii, 88.
[36] Journal, iii, 307.
[37] Journal, iii, 365, see also Letters, ii, 98.
[38] Journal, vii, 128.

[33] Letters, vi, 224.
[35] Letters, vii, 94.

[39] See above, p. 9.

By 1760, at the latest—so it seems to us—Wesley could easily have organized and regulated his local preachers. The fact that he did not do this, and that within five years of his death his followers had to do it, can only be ascribed to a personal reluctance on his part. The omission of mention of local preachers in the Deed of Declaration of 1784 is sufficient indication that Wesley did not regard local preachers as indispensable to the Connexion; and this is all the more remarkable when it is remembered that among those early local preachers were men like Dr James Whitehead, Wesley's personal physician and biographer, Dr James Hamilton, and Squire Brackenbury of Raithby Hall, Lincolnshire.

The truth is that it was not until the beginning of the nineteenth century, when Methodism had developed its own ways of worship, built its own chapels and, in towns and villages up and down the land, was demanding the services of preachers for as many as seven out of ten of its pulpits, that there emerges an organized body of Methodist Local Preachers. It had to wait even longer before these men were carefully trained and their studies supervised and Local Preachers affairs judged to be of sufficient importance to merit the setting up of a separate Connexional Department. But to return to the early days—after the death of Wesley, the local preachers were gradually brought within the organization and discipline of the Connexion. As Methodism developed, assuming the functions and duties of a Church with regular worship, and administration of the sacraments, local preachers were in increasing demand to fill the pulpits. It was the 1796 rules that first brought them officially within the constitution of the Connexion. The following Conference, it is interesting to note, referred to 'our worthy brethren, the Local Preachers whom, considered as a body, we greatly respect'—which is perhaps a sop to mitigate, if not to justify, the discipline which the previous Conference had found necessary to enforce.

To continue the history of that noble band of worthy brethren into the Methodism of today, where they play a vital role; or to follow their work in other Methodist bodies; or to trace their contribution to the society in which they have lived—is not within the scope of this article. All we have been able to do is to show how the Local Preacher has emerged, and been recognized in the pattern of Methodism—at first somewhat reluctantly, but later so inevitably that if his services were withdrawn today, three out of every four pulpits would be without a preacher next Sunday.

ADDITIONAL NOTE

Who was the first Methodist Lay Preacher? This honour is usually given to Thomas Maxfield, and the story is related of his preaching at the Foundery in early 1742.[40] Wesley was angry at Maxfield's presumption but the rebuke he received from his mother marked one of the turning points in his thinking, 'John, take care what you do with respect to that young man, for he is as surely called of God to preach as you are. Examine what have been the fruits of his preaching, and hear him yourself.' This certainly breached Wesley's unexamined assumption that preaching ought to be done only by ordained clergy, and prepared the way for the army of lay preachers which were later to be employed in the Methodist Revival.

On the other hand, in his Journal for Thursday, 9th September, 1790, Wesley speaks of Joseph Humphreys as 'the first lay preacher that assisted me in England in the year 1738'—but Humphreys was a Moravian and had been so since before Wesley's conversion. In an article in *The Proceedings of the Wesley Historical Society*[41] on 'Early Methodism in Bristol', the Rev. W. A. Goss claims that John Cennick was Wesley's first lay preacher, for he was employed as early as June 1739 in preaching to Kingswood colliers. This is supported by Tyerman,[42] so on balance of evidence it is perhaps right to regard John Cennick as the first Methodist Lay Preacher.[43]

[40] Tyerman, L.: *Life and Times of John Wesley*, i, 369.
[41] Vol. xix, 165.
[42] Op. cit., i, 274.
[43] On the whole question see also Church, L. F.: *More about the Early Methodist People*, p. 100.

2. Learning from the Saints

By the REV. FRANCIS B. JAMES

IF a preacher is to be able continually to give out to others, it is obviously necessary that he himself be continually taking in. And a preacher's reading is one important means of that inward replenishment. 'Reading maketh a full man,' says Bacon in a famous essay, Conference (or discussion) a ready man, Writing an exact man.'

In the pages that follow, a preacher's diligent and constant reading of the Bible may surely be assumed. Daily Bible reading should still be part of the rule of life for the Christian, even more for the Christian preacher and teacher. He should be, what John Wesley himself chose to be, as he says in words which every local preacher has presumably read, in the preface to the *Standard Sermons*, 'homo unius libri'—a man of one book. But, as John Wesley's own example and constant precept indicates, he must not be a man who reads one book only, but one for whom all other books are read by the light of the one Book, brought to its test, and read with the desire by its aid to understand that one Book more perfectly. Nor need anything be said here about a preacher's general theological reading. He will desire to read books about the Bible—commentaries and the literature of exposition. He will seek also for books that explore the meaning of the Christian faith, that set forth its answers to the agelong questions of the mind and show its relevance to the problems of the modern world.

But there is one special field of reading for which these present pages are a plea, and to which they may perhaps in some measure be a guide and help. There is what is generally described as 'spiritual reading' or the literature of devotion. Just as a medical student, after his years of study in the theory of medicine and healing, prepares himself in a more immediate way for his chosen career by the time he spends in hospital, and just as the doctor is still learning all through his years of practice, so he who would by his preaching minister to the spiritual health of others—applying to human needs the Gospel remedies, bringing men's souls to full growth and perfect soundness—will do well to read the books in which experienced Christians have shared with the world their own experience, shown to others what they themselves have discovered in God and His saving grace.

Saint Teresa says somewhere that those who would keep in touch with God must be much in the company of God's friends. And long before her, a wise Psalmist had said, 'I am a companion of those that fear Thee'. We too can be in the company of God's friends as we read some of what may be called the classics of devotion, books that men have written out of their own hearts, and in which they have passed on to others the lessons they themselves have learned. A few of these great Christian classics are familiar by name to most of us, but it is to be feared that they are less known and read today than in earlier times. They are more praised than really read; we treat them with respect, but do not make them companions of our way. Even such a book as Bunyan's *Pilgrim's Progress* is, it is to be feared, seldom read today. If it is thought of at all, it is dismissed as a 'children's book', though few even of the children of this generation know the story of Christian and those whom he met on his journey. But Bunyan's immortal allegory is much more than a children's book, much more even than one of the supreme achievements in English literature. It can still be a guide along the spiritual journey, from the City of Destruction, all through the perils and the comforts of the way, to the banks of that river on whose further side is the Celestial City.

Or there is that other book whose name is known surely to most Christians, Thomas à Kempis' *Imitation of Christ*, or *The Christian Pattern*, as John Wesley always called it. This classic of mediaeval monastic religion has its own message for our modern age. It could speak to men and women of today, as clearly and as arrestingly as it spoke to Maggie Tulliver in George Eliot's *The Mill on the Floss*, when she found the shabby little brown volume, with its pages marked by some long-dead reader, among a bundle of old books in the attic of the mill-house.

These two, and others of the great spiritual classics, are still available and easily accessible. Some are even included in the Penguin Books, and other series of 'paper-backs'. There one can find at least two of the great spiritual autobiographies. There is *The Confessions of St Augustine*, that thrilling story of God's pursuit and capture of a reluctant soul. And there is *The Life of Saint Teresa, written by herself*, a book discursive perhaps, but deeply moving, the inner story of surely the greatest woman in

Spanish history, an active reformer in the religious life of her time and country, and a great pioneer along the Way of Prayer.

Such great spiritual autobiographies as these, or as John Bunyan's *Grace Abounding to the Chief of Sinners*, may lead the reader on to other famous works of spiritual direction, like William Law's *Serious Call to a Devout and Holy Life*, a book which in his early manhood contributed to the shaping of John Wesley. It is true that after his evangelical conversion Wesley broke from Law's influence and criticized his teaching as gravely defective. Yet he never ceased to acknowledge his own indebtedness to Law or to commend the *Serious Call* to the Methodist people. Law's book also is available now in a paper-back edition, published by the Epworth Press. With it may be classed St Francis de Sales' *Introduction to the Devout Life*, an attractive and beautiful product of Seventeenth Century French devotion. Or, for those who would travel in the realms of gold, there are the mediaeval English mystics, Richard Rolle, Walter Hilton, and, best of all, Julian of Norwich's *Revelations of Divine Love*, a rich treasure indeed, in which one great lover of Jesus speaks to those who read it of her converse with Him whom she calls 'our courteous Lord'.

In such books—and he who begins to name them knows hardly where to end—the saints have mapped out for us that 'country afar beyond the stars' of which Henry Vaughan (*MHB* 466) teaches us to sing, a country not in this physical universe at all, but accessible to the spirit, a country, as Walter Hilton says, the way to which is run, 'not by paces of feet, but by desires of the heart'. The writers of such books are spiritual pioneers, pathfinders who come back to tell us where they have travelled, and to assure us that the treasures of that goodly land are for us also to find and to possess. Sometimes we cannot fully understand what they are saying. The things of which they try to tell are really too great for speech. But even their stammered tidings stir our hearts as we listen; for there is something within us that answers to their words, something that tells us that the land of which they speak is our own home, our native land. We are like exiles who on a foreign shore hear again the almost forgotten language of home.

It would be very good for any preacher—or indeed for any earnest Christian—to take at least, or as a beginning, one of these great spiritual classics, these books of the soul, and persevere with it, steep himself in its spirit, and put himself to school with it, get it right into his own mind and heart. Incidentally, such an attempt would be in harmony with John Wesley's own example and constant counsel. He was always insistent that his preachers must be readers, and he did all he could to make the range of their reading as wide as possible. Almost the first of John Wesley's many publications, issued in 1735, before his mission to Georgia and before his evangelical conversion, was a revised translation of à Kempis, and to the end of his life he continued to commend that book to his people. One of Wesley's most ambitious literary ventures was what he called 'The Christian Library'. This he published, during the space of several years, in fifty small and well-printed volumes, gathering together what he regarded as the best theological and devotional literature then available in English, selected, abridged, and, where he thought it necessary, revised by himself. *The Christian Library* was certainly not a financially rewarding publication, though early in the Nineteenth Century it was re-issued in thirty larger volumes. But it was an endeavour to encourage and assist the Methodist preachers to read. Wesley urged that in all the principal preaching places *The Christian Library* should be provided for the preachers, presumably local as well as itinerant!

The Christian Library is now, of course, completely out of date. Probably no one will ever again read steadily through the whole of those many volumes; though one could imagine a much worse choice for the proverbial desert island library! It is heavily weighted with Seventeenth and Eighteenth Century English theology, both Anglican and Puritan. But one thing *The Christian Library* does reveal, and that is the wide range of Wesley's own reading and the catholicity of his spirit. He includes extracts from the post-Apostolic Fathers, from the hermits of the Egyptian Deserts, and from the literature both of mediaeval and later monasticism. Some of Brother Lawrence's letters on the Practice of the Presence of God are included, something of Spanish mysticism, and also of the Seventeenth Century Cambridge Platonists. John Wesley could recognize everywhere the one central faith and the common experience that bind all real Christians into one, however different may be their modes of Church organization or even their ways of worship.

So many others too, in later times or in our own day, have written of the Christian religion in terms not of theology but of experience. One can only here mention such writings as the almost forgotten but richly rewarding books of Dora Greenwell, *The Patience of Hope, Two Friends*, and *Colloquia Crucis*; and such teachers too, of our own day, as Evelyn Underhill—with her *Concerning the Inner Life* and *The House of the Soul*; and Olive Wyon, in *The School of Prayer* and *The Altar Fire*; and our own Dr Sangster—especially in his studies in Christian Sanctity, *The Path to Perfection* and *The Pure in Heart*, and in his *Secret of Radiant Life*.

One other name may be mentioned here, because his writings, long almost unknown, have deeply influenced some of the spiritual teachers of today. P. J. de Caussade was a French Jesuit priest of the Eighteenth Century. After his death his teaching was gathered together into a book called *Self-Abandonment to Divine Providence*. In this, and in his collected *Spiritual Letters*, his characteristic ideas are expressed: the idea of faith as a continuous abandonment to the Will of God as revealed in the circumstances and events of daily life, and the thought of a 'moment-by-moment' union with God, finding Him in the here-and-now, or, to use de Caussade's own phrase, 'the Sacrament of the Present Moment'. Those who are familiar with Dr Sangster's later books will recognize how deeply our beloved Methodist saint and teacher had drunk in from de Caussade.

This may be an appropriate point at which to face one question that may arise in the mind of anyone who begins to explore the literature of devotion. Many of the most widely known and influential of these 'spiritual classics' come from pre-Reformation times and reflect the beliefs and spirit of their age and place. And even the best devotional literature of more recent times and of our own day belongs very largely to what is called—though it is a grave misuse of language—the 'Catholic' rather than the 'Protestant' side of the barrier which so tragically divides the Church of Christ.

If that be so, perhaps one has penitently to recognize the fact that in the past, and it may be also in the present, there has been in some ways more care on the other side of that great divide than among 'Protestants' for the development and culture of the inward life. The monasteries and convents of the pre-Reformation time were, at least at their best, schools of prayer and centres of spiritual life, as are many of the religious orders, both Roman and non-Roman, of today. The great rediscovery of the Reformation was the doctrine of Justification by Faith alone. The great note that was sounded afresh in the Methodist revival was the note of Evangelism, the offer to every man of a new birth, a present salvation. But have we sufficiently remembered that the newborn soul needs to be nurtured and fed, needs to grow up into full Christian manhood? Indeed, if we have failed there we have been unfaithful to our own beginnings, for the Methodist message of Christian Perfection or Perfect Love should have made us more careful for the growth of these newborn souls.

We need not be too greatly surprised if sometimes those whose Christian faith and ways of worship are very different, and even by our standards, in error, have in other ways so much to teach us. Rather let us, who ourselves have treasures that we hope one day to bring into the common store of the Church, be ready to accept from these others all that they have to give us, all the fruit of their experience, all that they know of the soul's life in Christ. And, most of all, let us rejoice, as the Wesleys did, that the saints, 'Catholic' or 'Protestant', are already one family in Christ. They speak the same language, recognize one another when they meet and see in one another's faces the same likeness; for all alike are mirrors of the same Holiness and Perfection.

Some of these saints and spiritual directors do more than point us along the heavenly road; they provide for us more definite and specific help in our own devotions. There are some devout and earnest Christians who find no help at all in books of private prayers and meditations, just as liturgical forms in public worship seem for some to be a hindrance and not a help. But there are others who are grateful to any who will offer them words to take with them into the secret place of prayer. Of all such helps to prayer available in the English language, none probably is better known than the *Private Devotions* of Lancelot Andrewes, Bishop of Winchester in the early Seventeenth Century. This book, first published after his death, was compiled through many years by Andrewes himself, for his own use; and the original manuscript was, as a contemporary witness reports, 'slubbered with his own pious hands and watered with his own penitential tears'. The book is made up of carefully considered and detailed forms of prayer for each day of the week, together with other devotions for morning and evening, and for many circumstances and occasions. They may at times seem over-elaborated and even artificial, but the more they are studied and used the more the reader will feel— as said one of the present writer's friends, to whom he had given a copy of Andrewes' book—that it is 'not a book, but a life'. Alexander Whyte said that to pray with Lancelot Andrewes for a week was to pray with him all one's life. Certainly our prayers may be lifted to a higher level as we kneel with Andrewes in adoration, our penitence deepened as with his candle we search our own hearts, our thanksgivings enlarged as he teaches us to reckon up God's mercies towards us, our sense of others' claim upon our prayers quickened as we join with him in the wide sweep of his intercession.

There are still many for whom Andrewes is a daily companion for the time of prayer. But probably for many modern people there is more help to be found in such a book as John Baillie's *Diary of Private Prayer*. This well-known book, first published in 1936, has gone through many editions, and has been greatly blessed. In it Dr Baillie provided prayers for use in the morning and evening of each day in the month—or rather aids to prayer; for, as the author says, 'they are not intended to form the whole of the morning's or evening's devotions, or to take the place of more individual prayers for oneself or for others'. Then, among other helps to prayer which many in our own time have learned to treasure, there are those two beautiful and deeply reverent books of Eric Milner-White, Dean of York, *My God my Glory* and *A Procession of Passion Prayers*. And, of course, many of our readers will already have made acquaintance with our own Leslie Weatherhead's book, *A Private House of Prayer*. The scheme of this book is original. Dr Weatherhead thinks of the various elements that constitute prayer as being rooms in the soul's personal House of Prayer. It is a seven-roomed house that he visualizes, and he names those rooms in order as (1) Affirmation of the Divine Presence, (2) Adoration, Praise, and Thanksgiving, (3) Confession, Forgiveness, and Unloading (the last word suggesting the relief with which the forgiven soul lays down its burden), (4) Reception, in which the soul consciously claims from God His offered grace, (5) Petition, (6) Intercession, and (7) Meditation. For each day in a month Dr Weatherhead furnishes these seven rooms with material, often of his own fashioning, but often drawn from the classic treasures of devotion and from modern Christian testimony and experience, but all designed to help the devout soul in these successive acts and exercises of prayer.

Such books of private devotion—and there are others that might be mentioned—will be for many preachers a real help in the maintenance and enrichment of their own inner life of prayer. But though that is their primary purpose, their use will also be of great assistance to the preacher, in his responsibility for leading the prayers of others. They will give worthier language, deeper depth of meaning and wider range to the worship in which one man or woman is called to speak to God on behalf of others as well as to speak to others on behalf of God.

But, when speaking or writing of such books, it must not be forgotten that—next, of course, to the Bible—the best of all such helps to prayer is a good hymn-book. It is much to be regretted that so many church-going folk today think of their hymn-book only as something to be taken to church on Sunday—as one takes one's envelope for the collection—or worse still, as something that one keeps in the pew, or borrows from the steward at the door! The Christian's hymn-book should be the daily companion, with his Bible, of his times of prayer. Nor is it denominational pride that makes one feel that there is no modern English hymn-book more suited to that office than our own Methodist Hymn-book, especially having regard to the large proportion in it of hymns and translations actually by the Wesleys themselves. Even more fortunate are those Methodists who possess and use the old 'Wesleyan' Hymn-book, as published in 1780, under the title, *A Collection of Hymns for the use of the People called Methodists*—a collection that remained almost unaltered, though with successive supplements, until the whole book was recast in 1904. That old book was indeed, as John Wesley wrote in his famous 1780 Preface, 'a little body of practical and experimental divinity'. As its Table of Contents clearly indicates, the greater part of it consisted of hymns for those seeking salvation, for penitent sinners, for back-sliders convinced and recovered, and for believers under various conditions and at various stages of their pilgrim way: 'Believers Rejoicing, Fighting, Praying, Watching, Working, Suffering, Seeking for Full Redemption', and for those to whom that gift of Perfect Love had been in some degree given. Even in the Hymn-book that we now use, so much of the spirit of that early time remains as to justify Wesley's question as to where, in any such book, can be found 'so distinct and full an account of Scriptural Christianity, such a declaration of the heights and depths of religion, or such clear directions for making your calling and election sure, and for perfecting holiness in the fear of God'. It can be to the user, as Wesley again says, 'a means of raising or quickening the spirit of devotion, of confirming his faith, of enlivening his hope, and of kindling and increasing his love to God and man'. Such a hymn-book is a treasure indeed, and a companion even more for the inner room and the quiet hour than for the place and the time of public worship.

Thus far we have been concerned with reading that is specifically devotional, the classics of the spiritual life, the books that offer direct help in prayer, the books that explore the possibilities of the soul's life in God. The preacher will do well to turn his attention to such reading, and to persevere therein. But there is another range of reading that, for the present writer, and probably for many others, is equally rich in value for the culture of the soul. There are books in which we have not so much formal exposition of the meaning of the spiritual life, nor language for our prayers and praises, but rather the spontaneous and unstudied expression of the spiritual life in the form of intimate and personal letters. In past ages, and in our own time, there have been great Christians whose letters to others have been so valued for their help and guidance in spiritual things that those letters have been treasured and preserved by those to whom they were written, and presently gathered together and made accessible to a wider circle.

Some, of course, of the books that rank as spiritual classics are of this description: *The Letters of Samuel Rutherford*, for instance. An English merchant, travelling in Scotland about 1650, told of various preachers he had heard there, and among them, 'a little fair man, who showed me the loveliness of Christ'. And Samuel Rutherford, thrust out of his pulpit in Scotland's struggle against the attempt to force prelacy and the English Prayer Book upon her Church, has been, through his Letters, showing Christ's loveliness ever since. For some, his letters are too emotional, too unreserved, expressing the soul's love for Christ too much in the language of human affection—though seldom more so than is warranted by Scripture! But for others, Samuel Rutherford can be an unfailing guide to the heights and depths of the soul's life in Christ. From a different part of Christ's Household, and expressing in different ways the same love and trust and obedience, are the published letters of two French bishops of the same century. Francis de Sales and Francis Fénelon were both wise and trusted spiritual guides in their own time to many, and, through their published letters, to many others in the ages following.

The Letters of Thomas Erskine of Linlathen, too, are a rich treasure to those who know them. Thomas Erskine, a Scottish laird, played a considerable part in the liberalizing of theology in England and Scotland in the Nineteenth Century. He was the trusted friend of such men as Thomas Chalmers and F. D. Maurice. His books, influential in their day, are now only of historical interest. But his *Letters* still stand to reveal the mind and heart of one for whom it was the spiritual and eternal world, the life in Christ, that alone gave meaning and value to life in this world of sense and time.

It would be a pity, too, if the *Letters of James Smetham* were to be altogether forgotten among us. For, in a way, this book is a kind of classic expression of Nineteenth Century English Methodism. James Smetham, cradled in Methodism, a minister's son, and a scholar at Woodhouse Grove, was an artist, a drawing-master for many years at Westminster Teacher Training College. He was a disciple and friend of John Ruskin, but also a Methodist class-leader and a prolific letter-writer. His *Letters*, gathered and published soon after his death, give many intimate and charming glimpses of the life of a London Methodist church in the latter part of last century. But they are also the unconscious self-portrait of a devout soul, clinging, through the storm and stress of a troubled life and the questionings and denials of the Victorian age, to the simple evangelical faith that he had received and whose power he had proved in his own soul.

Still nearer to our own time lived Forbes Robinson, a member of a distinguished Anglican family, whose *Letters to his Friends*—first printed privately soon after his death nearly sixty years ago, but afterwards made available to a wider public—surely takes rank as a modern spiritual classic. Forbes Robinson was a Cambridge don who exercised a great spiritual influence over the undergraduates of his time, and especially over those preparing for ordination. There must be others, besides the present writer, who are grateful to Dr Ferrier Hulme—that true Father-in-God to the probationers in his District—for introducing them, in their early ministry, to this then little-known book. Forbes Robinson's *Letters* are a revelation of a man to whom prayer was the breath of life, and who, by those letters, is still teaching others what the ministry of intercession can be.

Of some of the great spiritual teachers of recent times it is perhaps almost better for our purpose to read their published letters than to study their books: Evelyn Underhill, for instance, and her own great spiritual master, Baron von Hügel. In the posthumously published letters of the Baron, and especially in those written to, and gathered together by, his niece, Gwendolen Greene, we see that profound and widely influential Christian thinker as the simple and adoring child of his Heavenly Father, and the lover of his Lord. Other collections of 'spiritual letters' too may be mentioned here, such as those of Father R. M. Benson, the founder of the Society of St John the Evangelist at Cowley; Father Andrew, living and working in war-time among the poor of East London; and Dom John Chapman, Roman Catholic Abbot of Downside, whose *Spiritual Letters* have given guidance in the things of God to many readers beyond the bounds of his own Church.

So, in the letters of saintly men and women we can receive, as their own circles of friends received, refreshment and guidance in our spiritual pilgrimage. We can be indeed in company with God as we keep company with these His friends. But this is true also as we read the records of saintly lives. There are few kinds of literature more enjoyable than biography, or more profitable for the preacher. This is partly because biography is an inexhaustible source of illustration for the preacher's sermons! But it is also true that the kind of biography we have now in mind is profitable for the stirring of the preacher's devotion, and the deepening of his understanding of God's ways with the souls of men. 'God's Way with a Soul'—that was to have been the title of the auto- biography of which Horace Bushnell left only the beginning. And St Teresa tells us that when she wrote her own life-story she at first intended to call it, 'A Book of the Mercies of God'. Every biography that does more than record the outward events in the life of a Christian man or woman is the story of God's wise and merciful way with that particular soul.

There are some fairly recent biographies that are not only of absorbing interest but of real devotional value to the preacher. It has been seriously suggested that *The Life of Alexander Whyte* (G. F. Barbour) might well be made compulsory reading for a preacher in the early years of his ministry. There are those who read it again and again to be in company, not only with the greatest Scottish preacher of last generation, but with one who all his long life walked penitently and humbly with his God. The same is true in their measure of such biographies as those of Hudson Taylor, the founder of the China Inland Mission, of Mrs Howard Taylor, his daughter-in-law, of Amy Carmichael of Dohnavur, and of Temple Gairdner of Cairo, that missionary scholar-saint. Why is it, incidentally, that so many missionary biographies have so real a devotional value? Is it that the task to which these men and women devoted themselves drove them, more deeply than the rest of us, into the secret life with God?

Another richly rewarding biography of this kind is *The Life and Letters of Janet Erskine Stuart*, by Maud Monahan. Janet

Stuart was a Roman Catholic, the Superior-General in her later years of a women's religious order, the Society of the Sacred Heart. But no difference of Church attachment need come between any reader and this noble woman who, by her letters especially and out of her own rich spiritual life, was to many others—and still can be—a great teacher in the way of trust and love and obedience. And yet another biography, from the Protestant side, is Olive Wyon's *Radiant Freedom*, the story of Emma Pieczynska, a Swiss woman of whose troubled but victorious life Dr Wyon says, quoting from two of Emma's friends, 'Her life was illumined by the things of which she was deprived' and also 'She made magnificent bouquets of the refusals of God'.

We Methodists, while sharing in the riches of other parts of Christ's Holy Church, have also our own biographical classics. One book which, if not still in print, ought certainly to be re-issued, is the tender and appealing *Love and Life*, the book which, with filial piety and literary skill, Bardsley Brash wrote about his father. John Denholm Brash, alike in his eager and loving ministry and in his closing years of patient and cheerful suffering, was a living exposition of the Methodist doctrine of Perfect Love. Also, among our Methodist classics, must surely now be numbered Paul Sangster's biography of his father, *Doctor Sangster*, who, through that book, still offers to us the Christ whom he lived to preach. To read and to re-read such books—and those who read them once will surely want to re-read—is indeed to be in company with the friends of God, and by fellowship with them to be brought ever more deeply into the wonder of His friendship.

Of course, in this as in other fields of literature, each reader has to find his own way and follow where he is most drawn and helped. In a book to which Evelyn Underhill gave the appropriate title, *Mixed Pasture*, she quotes very characteristic words from her own great teacher, Baron von Hügel. The Baron says, 'I love to watch cows as they browse at the borders of fields, up against the hedges. They move along, with their great tongues drawing in just only what they can assimilate. Yes, but without stopping to snort defiantly against what does not thus suit them. So ought we to do.' This is specially true, as the Baron was suggesting, of the literature of devotion. It may be that a reader will find that some book which has meant much to others has little or nothing in it that he himself can receive. Then let him put it by, though not till he is sure that for him at least that particular spiritual herbage holds no nourishment. But let him go on tasting here and there till he finds, as he surely will, some rich pasture whereon his soul can feed. So will there come to the preacher, as in his spiritual reading he keeps company with one and another of the friends of God, a continual deepening and widening of his own religious life and experience. And so will his ministry to others be enriched, as he passes on to them what he himself is continually receiving.

ADDITIONAL NOTE

It may be that some who read the foregoing pages will be wondering how to gain access to some of the books that have been mentioned and commended here. Any good bookseller, of course, can give information as to whether, and at what price, any such book is now on sale. It is to be feared that many of the kind of books we have in mind are no longer in print and obtainable through the ordinary channels. The heavy cost of production makes it difficult for publishers to keep in print books for which there is no great or steady demand.

Nor are such books obtainable second-hand as readily as once they were. In the salvage drives of the War years much irreplaceable literature, of real value, must have been destroyed in haste and ignorance. Many books which thirty years ago were constantly seen in second-hand shops are now seldom to be found there. The 'twopenny box' no longer exists, and the 'sixpenny shelf' has now few joyful surprises! However, it is wise to keep an eye on the second-hand book shops. And let it be remembered that at the Epworth Press (25–35 City Road, E.C.1) there is a second-hand department where one can count on special knowledge of, and interest in, the kind of books we now have in mind.

But it is one of the encouraging signs of our time that there is a renewed demand for some of the spiritual classics. This is evidenced by the fact, mentioned already, that several of these are now obtainable in the various cheap 'paper-back' series. The Student Christian Movement Press also has 'A Treasury of Christian Books', including Bunyan's *Grace Abounding*, Bishop Andrewes' *Private Prayers*, and *Selected Letters of Samuel Rutherford*. Another selection from Rutherford's *Letters* is one of the Epworth Press 'Devotional Books', in which series also is published one of Dora Greenwell's books, *Two Friends*, introduced by Henry Bett, to whom Dora Greenwell was 'one of the greatest devotional writers in the English language'. Another famous series, long unobtainable, but now being gradually re-issued, is Methuen's 'Library of Devotion' including *The Confessions of St Augustine*, *The Imitation of Christ*, Law's *Serious Call*, Andrewes' *Private Prayers*, and Molinos' *Spiritual Guide*. There is yet another series of attractive pocket-sized books, 'The Orchard Books', published by Burns Oates. This includes another translation of Augustine's *Confessions*, Francis de Sales' *Introduction to the Devout Life*, and also *Revelations of Divine Love*—though the best edition of the Lady Julian's book still remains that edited by Grace Warrack and published by Methuen.

But, as has already been said, any competent bookseller has at his command full information as to books that are now in print. And, for the rest, there are still the second-hand shops! The best books are still to be found by those who will search for them. Great is the reward of those who find! And even in the seeking for such 'goodly pearls', there is a joy.

3. The Preacher's Use of Words[1]

By the REV. J. ALAN KAY, M.A., Ph.D.

THERE is no doubt that our congregations often feel that the pulpit is somehow out of touch with ordinary living. There are more reasons for this than one, and not all of them are discreditable to the preacher, but Dr Sangster in his Joseph Smith Memorial Lecture suggests that one of the reasons is that preachers sometimes use *one vocabulary for daily life and another for the conduct of worship*. The difference between them, he says, was brought home to the people of St Louis with startling suddenness a while ago. A fervent religious service came to its crashing close, vocabulary and intonation being both in the manner felt to be fitting for the 'Pulpit of the Air'. Indeed, the unctuous overtones still hung on the atmosphere when the minister (unaware that he had not been cut off) was heard to remark in a natural but jubilant tone to his companions in the studio: 'Well, boys, we hit it right on the nose that time.'

It is of course true that in the pulpit we expect a certain dignity of utterance, and that therefore pulpit language ought to be different from the informal colloquialism of everyday conversation. A preacher who used undignified language would be just as mistaken as one who conducted the service in the brief shorts and open-necked shirt of a summer cyclist. It is also true that in the pulpit we cannot help but use a number of technical words which belong to our subject. If men go to listen to somebody speaking about electricity, they must expect to hear about amps and anodes, contacts and currents, valves and volts; and, similarly, if they go to church they must not be surprised if the preacher uses his own set of technical terms and talks about grace, righteousness, glory, and faith. These are part of the necessary apparatus for talking and even thinking deeply about Christianity, and if people reckon to be interested in the subject it is reasonable to expect them to make themselves acquainted with its terms. But allowing for all this, it is still true that pulpit language is often too much removed from that of ordinary life.

[1] This material, drawn from three articles previously written by Dr Kay, was being revised and prepared by him for this *Preacher's Handbook* at the time of his death.

Very often it is *archaic*. When one remembers the beauty and influence of the Authorized Version, it is easy enough to understand how this comes about, but it is a mistake all the same. Why should we say 'oftentimes', 'nigh', and 'eventide' in the pulpit, when in ordinary speech we say 'often', 'near', and 'evening'? No one, reporting a local cricket match, would say: 'The batsman oftentimes drove the ball through the covers,' or arrange to meet a friend at the station 'nigh the bookstall', or propose 'to spend an eventide at the pictures'. Similarly, when our children in bed are afraid of the dark, they do not ask their mothers to 'abide' with them, and when we see someone knocked down by a car, we are not 'sore' upset. 'Manifold' is another of these pulpit words. We may use it as the name of a valley, or part of a machine, or with reference to the intestines (especially, says the dictionary, the third stomach of a ruminant!), but it is not the ordinary word for 'many'; we should not describe the weeds in our garden as being manifold, and there is no reason why in the pulpit we should apply it to temptations or troubles. Nor is it really natural to 'vouchsafe' or to refer to people who are ill as 'the sick'.

Some pulpit words and phrases are undesirable merely because they have been *overused*. It would be a great relief if for a few years we heard no 'clarion calls' (how many members of our congregations have ever heard a clarion, anyway?), if we did not find ourselves 'at the cross-roads', if memories were not 'fragrant', and if nothing 'bore eloquent testimony'. It would be a good thing, too, if at our funeral services we recognized that men died, and did not merely 'pass away' or 'fall asleep' or (very odd this) 'fall *on* sleep'. And how pleasant it would be if we heard nothing about 'aggressive evangelism' for a long time. Indeed, we ought not to hear of it at all, for 'aggressive' and its associated words always have a bad sense. To be aggressive is to be offensive, aggression is an unprovoked attack, and an aggressor is one who begins a quarrel. People who are aggressive always make us want to resist, and if they were let loose as evangelists they would do more harm than good.

Many pulpit words are wrong because they are *pretentious*. In ordinary life people play and sing, but in church they 'preside at the organ' and 'render' the anthem. Most of us go to work every day, but one would suppose from many a sermon that what we went to was our 'labour' or 'toil'. If on a day off we are going to a football match we perhaps arrange to meet our friends, but if it is a church outing we do nothing so simple—we 'foregather'.

Every Sunday stewards 'wait upon' congregations to receive their offerings as though they were making a formal and elegant call upon a member of the nobility in the eighteenth century. In ordinary life an action may 'bring honour to' or 'reflect credit on', but in the pulpit it is always apt to 'redound'. When the typist fails to arrive at the office on a Monday morning we suppose that she must be ill, but if she fails to come to the service on a Sunday evening, we tend to think that she is 'laid aside', like an article in a Christmas Club that is being kept until its purchaser has saved enough money to pay for it.

Language like this is one of the things that give an air of un-reality to our services. It takes religion out of the realm of real living and gives it the feel of being a thing by itself, separated from ordinary life, and therefore largely irrelevant.

Our choice of words can, therefore, build up barriers between us and those around us, and obscure the very things we want to make plain. This is ironic, for God has given us the gift of speech as a means of communication, a way of building not walls but bridges. Our words should be vehicles, not obstacles. It is vitally important that we choose and use them aright. This is true for everyone; but it is especially true for the preacher.

* * *

A preacher is a man of many words—it is indeed alarming to think how many he must use during his ministry. That should mean that words are precious to him, that he respects them, uses them with care, and develops that skill which is necessary to make them produce the effects he wants. They are, after all, immensely powerful; they can comfort the heart or break it, rouse to battle or lull to sleep, enlighten with the truth or deceive with a lie, point a man to heaven or lead him to hell, be an inspiration which lingers in his mind or become a curse which he tries to turn out of it in vain.

A. J. Gossip, speaking to preachers, once said: 'Style is not idle. It is power. Time spent upon it is not wasted, the mere suggestion is a crime. For a phrase, an image, an apt adjective, may bring home to some needy soul a whole new side of truth, may make it feel God very near, may win it for the Master. It is often through such things that these great matters happen.' We do not apologize, therefore, for writing about words.

Matthew Arnold professed to think that the 'only secret of style' was to 'have something to say and say it as clearly as you can'. But if he meant that nothing more could or needed to be said about it, he was clearly wrong. The fact is that style is not a matter of mere clarity, and that even if it were, clarity is a thing that has to be learnt. In newspapers and conversation we are so used to reading and hearing poor, and even bad style, that we all tend to become infected with it and to reproduce its blemishes in our own speech. We all need to take some pains to cultivate a style that is good. Fortunately it is possible to lay down a number of simple rules about the matter. Their observance will not make anyone into a stylistic genius, but it will enable the ordinary preacher—so long as he has something important to say—to make his sermons clear instead of muddy, vigorous instead of flabby, comely instead of ugly, and interesting instead of dull.

Most of these rules have often been stated, but not all of them in connection with preaching, though they apply just as much to the spoken word as to the written one. It will therefore be salutary to look at them again with preaching particularly in mind. Unfortunately they have often been stated in a way which is too absolute—'Use A and not B'. But they cannot be put in that form without being misleading, and we must try to express them more carefully. There will not be room to mention them all, so we will concentrate for the time being on the negative and therefore more easy ones.

The first rule is: *Do not use a long word when a short one will do*. The second is: *Do not use a Latin or French word when a Saxon one will do*. These two rules overlap a good deal, and therefore it will be convenient to consider them together. They remind us that for ordinary purposes it is better to 'begin' than to 'commence' (Genesis does not say, 'In the commencement God created the heaven and the earth'), to 'give' than to 'donate' (Acts does not say, 'It is more blessed to donate than to receive'), to 'help' than to 'assist', to 'use' than to 'utilize', to be 'able to walk' than to be 'capable of locomotion', to 'see whether Mrs Jones is in' than to 'ascertain whether she is upon the premises'. Similarly it is a mistake to use 'prior to' for 'before', 'following' for 'after', and 'currently' for 'now'. Dr Johnson once said of a certain play, 'It has not wit enough to keep it sweet', and then, translating this judgement into Johnsonese, he added under his breath, 'It has not sufficient vitality to preserve it from putrefaction'—but his first thoughts were best. That, incidentally, is very largely why today we often quote his talk but seldom his writings. The short word is simple and direct; the Saxon word is natural and unpretentious; both of them are to be preferred to the long and the latinized, which so easily sounds difficult, pompous, or vain.

The third rule is very similar to the first two: *Do not use a long phrase when a short one will do*, or a short phrase when a single word will do. A. P. Herbert, in a radio talk, once pointed out that the sense of Nelson's famous message, 'England expects that every man will do his duty', might be conveyed by the words, 'This country anticipates that, in the current emergency, personnel will implement their obligations according to the functions appertaining to their respective age groups.' It is safe to say, however, that if Nelson had said that, no one would have bothered to remember it. Another example may be found in the comment which was made about the inscription which Canning prepared for Pitt's monument in London's Guildhall. He used the expression 'he died poor', and one of the aldermen, thinking that was too ordinary, wanted to substitute 'he expired in indigent circumstances'. But how strong and moving is the ordinary phrase, and how cold and weak the alderman's proposed substitute!

If we follow this rule, we shall recognize that it is better to have 'full time work' than 'work on a full time basis', to 'play games' than to 'indulge in recreational facilities', and to 'receive' than to 'be made the recipient of' (Ananias did not tell Saul of Tarsus that the Lord had sent him that he might be made the recipient of his sight). We shall also look with grave suspicion at all such phrases as 'in connection with', 'in regard to', 'in respect of', 'in the case of', 'in relation to', and 'with reference to'; they can nearly always be replaced by 'to', 'with', 'for', 'by', 'of', or 'about'. Shakespeare is generally a very good model, and he did not write any plays with the titles 'Measure in relation to Measure', 'The Comedy in respect of Errors', or 'Much ado with regard to Nothing'.

The fourth rule partly overlaps the third: *Do not use a verb and a noun, particularly an abstract noun, when you can use a verb by itself*. The parable of the Prodigal Son does not begin, 'A certain man was the possessor of two sons'; it says, much more simply and directly, he 'had' them. Jesus did not say, 'Make application and you shall receive; make a search and you shall find; give some knocks and the door shall be opened'.

The fifth rule is: *Do not use the passive voice when the active will do*. The passive is stationary and sometimes cumbersome, so it is generally more direct and more vivid to use the active. 'They killed him' has more life about it than 'He was killed', and our speech ought to be lively even when we are talking about death. Similarly, 'we must' is more effective than 'it is necessary that we should'. In the subway in New York there are notices saying, 'Expectoration is forbidden'; but apart from the fact that 'expectoration' is not a word which most of the people who indulge in it would recognize, it is clearly better to use the active voice and say 'Do not spit'.

The sixth rule is of rather a different kind: *Do not use a stale phrase when a fresh one will do.* That, indeed, is a very mild way of putting it, because a fresh phrase is something to be delighted in, not merely accepted; and a stale phrase is generally an abomination. However, it is sometimes possible to bring to life a phrase that is not merely stale but dead, and so it is right to phrase this rule in the same way as the others. Preachers, alas, often seem to take refuge in clichés, phrases which, although they were once original and full of vitality, have become stale through much use. We ought not to hear from the pulpit—or for that matter from anywhere else—such expressions as 'conspicuous by its absence', 'in our day and generation', 'the answer was in the negative', 'the iron entered his soul', and all those other phrases which so easily spring to the lips of speakers who are not thinking very hard, and so completely lull the minds of the hearers that they stop thinking altogether. More especially should we avoid them when they are religious—in the Church of England, 'Our blessed Lord'; and in the Free Churches, 'We thank Thee that once again we are privileged to gather within the sanctuary.' When we preach we want our people to see things anew, to hear them as though for the first time, to taste the goodness of God in all its freshness, to find that the word of the Lord is not something that belongs to the stale past but is living and contemporary; we want them to be lifted out of the old ruts of thought and feeling and behaviour where they have got stuck, and to move forward— sometimes in a completely new direction. They will not do all this if we serve up God's new wine in old bottles which they have seen on the table over and over again. Moreover, when we try to do so, we give ourselves away and show that we ourselves are living on old experiences; if our experience was new we should want new and personal phrases in which to describe it.

We said at the beginning that it was easy to phrase rules of style in a way which made them too rigid. That is why we have put them in the form, 'Do not use A when B will do.' For of course B will very often not do at all. The effect of following the rules we have mentioned will be to make our speech more simple and clear (and therefore as a rule more forceful and interesting), but simplicity and clarity are not the only qualities a preacher seeks. He wants to express not only his thoughts but also his feelings, and for that purpose he will often choose a word or phrase which he would otherwise reject.

Take, for example, our first two rules about using words which are simple and Saxon. According to them, we ought to prefer the word 'woolly' to the word 'flocculent', and we should generally be right. But when Sir Winston Churchill was writing the first volume of his Second World War, he evidently found that 'woolly' did not fully express his feelings about certain people's mental processes, and he therefore called them 'flocculent', thus expressing a stronger contempt for them than 'woolly' would have conveyed. Charles Wesley, as has often been pointed out, knew very well the value of a long Latin word. There is a feeling of absolute finality about 'With inextinguishable blaze'; it is so confident, so certain, that any idea that the flame might conceivably be quenched is altogether ruled out. Some hymn-books (incredibly) have altered the line to 'With ever bright, undying blaze', but although that means very much the same, it feels totally different. We have quoted the Bible in support of short Saxon words, but we must not forget such a passage as I Corinthians 15, with its talk of 'bodies celestial and bodies terrestrial', and the splendour of such a verse as 'For this corruptible must put on incorruption, and this mortal must put on immortality.' The New Testament in Basic English (falsely so called) may speak instead of 'bodies of heaven and bodies of earth', and may dim the glory of the resurrection by reducing the verse we have quoted to, 'For this body which comes to destruction will be made free from the power of death, and the man who is under the power of death will put on eternal life', but no one who conducts a funeral, we hope, will think of reading that.

These, however, are special cases, and they are found in the speech of men whose vocabulary is predominantly simple. They are not breaches of the rules as we have given them, but instances in which short and Saxon words cannot do what is required. The rule that they should be used where they can do so still holds. The same thing applies to the other rules. There are many occasions when it is good to use a long phrase, an abstract noun, or a verb in the passive voice, and there are even some, as we have already suggested, when it is effective for certain purposes to use a cliché. The point is that none of these things should be used when their alternatives will do; in fact if their alternatives do at all, they will do very much better.

The rules we have given may seem small, but it is astonishing how great is the effect of following them. Many a preacher, by writing out his sermons and then going through them with these rules in mind, altering his words and phrases where necessary, would increase the effectiveness of his preaching enormously. Important as these negative rules are, however, there are other positive ones which are even more important, and to these we must now turn.

*   *   *

The most important of the positive rules is 'Wherever possible, be concrete.' As Dr Maltby once wrote in his Thirty Concepts for Preachers, 'The abstract puffeth up: the concrete buildeth up.'

The Bible is a good guide here. It speaks of a Father but not of fatherhood, of children but not of childlikeness; it is full of concrete metaphors, similes, parables, examples. The sermons of great preachers are the same. If we analyse their most effective and luminous passages, we shall find that their power nearly always depends very much on concrete imagery.

One of the uses of metaphor and simile is that of maintaining interest. Everyone is interested in relationships, in fitting things together and finding links between them. That is why the scientist tries to find a common law which will explain many different facts, and why an artist makes the various objects in his picture fit together into a pattern; that is why we have conundrums which ask 'Why is A like B?' and why we laugh at puns and why we think the deliberate rejection of congruity is comic. Whenever we can link things together, whether in thought or appearance or sound, we are pleased. Metaphors and similes, therefore, even if they do nothing else, rouse and maintain interest.

In the course of his lectures on preaching, Phillips Brooks talks about the advantages and difficulties of planning sermons in a series. 'The only serious danger about a course of sermons', he says, 'is, that where the serpent grows too long it is difficult to have the vitality distributed through all his length, and even to his last extremity. Too many courses of sermons start with a very vital head, that draws behind it by and by a very lifeless tail. The head springs and the tail crawls, and so the beast makes no graceful progress.' This metaphor is not strictly necessary to the thought, and its elaboration is certainly mere ornament. Nevertheless, it is undeniably fascinating ornament, and we listen to what he has to say with increased interest because of the picture he draws of a reptile waving its head about and dragging its lifeless tail behind. Similarly, when Chesterton, referring to the fact that Bernard Shaw's view of life is incomplete, remarks that 'Shaw is like the Venus of Milo; all that there is of him is admirable', his reference to Greek statuary adds nothing to his logic but contributes a great deal to our interest.

Now it is part of the business of the preacher to rouse and maintain his congregation's interest, and the use of apt metaphors and similes is one of the things which help him to do it.

The value of concrete imagery, however, is not merely that it adds to the sermon's interest. The image helps the thought to penetrate the mind; it gives it a sharp point which can pierce the tough skin of indifference with which men protect themselves from the rough jostling of life. A. J. Gossip, speaking of Jesus, says, 'To us His life looks bleak and shivery and windswept, yet He was always blessing God for something; and so perfect was His obedience, that where you and I would have whimpered, or, at best, schooled ourselves to accept with lips bitten hard lest we cry out, Jesus was full of gratitude.' These pictures of one man shivering on a bleak and barren moor, and another biting his lips lest he groan with pain, thrust themselves into our minds where a plain statement would never have got across its threshold but, like a hawker, have been automatically turned away from the door. So when Jesus said, 'It is easier for a camel to go through the eye of a needle than for a rich man to enter into the Kingdom of Heaven', the metaphor gave His saying a cutting edge which enabled it to open a way into the listener's mind.

The greater ease with which a concrete statement enters the mind is partly due to its greater clarity; a picture is easier to grasp than an abstract idea. To say that the greatness of the sin of man is infinitely surpassed by the greatness of the love of Christ is to state the relationship between the two things in such a way that a man can see what it is only if he screws up his eyes a little and looks hard. To say, as Bunyan does, that the one is no more to the other than 'this little clot or stone before me is to this vast and wide field that here I see', is to make a dim and blurred idea suddenly come into focus, and to give it a sharp and definite shape. Similarly, when George Orwell, being deliberately obscure, paraphrases a biblical text in the words, 'Success or failure in competitive activities exhibits no tendency to be commensurate with innate capacity', it is difficult to recognize the verse, 'The race is not to the swift nor the battle to the strong', because the original is so clear and bright, and the paraphrase so muddy and dull.

Sometimes an image acts as a kind of argument. It has the effect of saying, 'What I am telling you is not impossible or irrational because it is a kind of thing which you are familiar with elsewhere', or 'We accept this general principle in other matters, why should we not accept it here?' Thus Fuller says, 'To clothe low-creeping matter with high-flown language is not fine fancy, but flat foolery. It rather loads than raises a wren, to fasten the feathers of an ostrich to her wings.' And we say immediately, 'Yes, of course.' If it had not been for his illustration, we might have felt inclined to dispute what he was saying, and to maintain that it might be a very good idea to clothe 'low-creeping matter' in a few fine words so as to give it a little more dignity; but his image conquers us. Similarly, when he points to the two proverbs, 'the throne is established by justice' and 'the throne is upholden by mercy', and says they 'speak no more contradiction, than he that said that the two opposite side walls of a house hold up the same roof', we see an argument for believing both together, because we are reminded that objects do sometimes need to be upheld by two things rather than by one. Again, one Easter Sunday H. L. Paget compared the cycle of the Church festivals to a dog with its bone. Of course, he said, the dog knows all along where the bone is, but he buries it for a bit because of the sheer joy that rediscovery brings. This illustration, says his biographer, 'sent his . . . churchwarden riding round his farmlands with a new understanding of Easter'.

Needless to say, an analogy is not *necessarily* an argument, and sometimes people are taken in by supposing it to be one when it is not. Nevertheless, it *may* be an argument, and a very strong and effective one, as when Jesus says, 'what man is there of you, who, if his son shall ask him for a loaf, will give him a stone; or if he shall ask for a fish, will give him a serpent? If ye then, being evil, know how to give good gifts unto your children, how much more shall your Father which is in heaven give good things to them that ask him?'

One of the difficulties of preaching, especially to those who are beginning, is that of amplification. It is not enough that the truth should be stated, not enough even that it should be stated interestingly and clearly and logically; it has to be talked about for a sufficient length of time for it to sink in; the congregation must be given the opportunity to digest it. Sermonic amplification can of course be ruinous if it is done in the wrong way, but that does not mean that there is not a right way of doing it, or that it is unnecessary. It was no doubt a cynic who said that a book should be solid, a lecture liquid, and a sermon gas; but the fact which he was caricaturing was nevertheless a real fact. A sermon, which the listener has to absorb while the words are being spoken, should not be as solid as a book, which the reader can follow as slowly as he wishes, stop and meditate upon as long as he desires, and read over again as often as he finds necessary. Now one of the best ways of amplifying is by the use of images.

A good example may be found in a sermon on 'the Son of man hath not where to lay his head', by Alexander Whyte. The preacher concludes by asking his congregation whether they are always ready to welcome Christ, and begs them to be prepared to receive Him this very night. It is a simple thought, but they have to be made to think about it long enough for it to sink in. He amplifies it therefore by elaborating a picture:

When a much-loved and long-expected friend knocks on our door we know his knock and we open the door and say to him, Even so, come quickly. We say, Come away, for I was just thinking about you when you knocked. I was just reading one of your old letters to occupy myself till you should knock. I could not sleep last night for dreaming about you: come away, come away. Sit up in that way for Him tonight. Expect Him this very night. Set a candle in your window for Him tonight. Have your door ajar for Him tonight.

The ideas of thinking about a friend and reading his letters, of course, suggests something about what waiting for Christ means, but the rest is amplification, and its main purpose is to give time for the idea to impress itself upon the mind and leave its mark there.

Concrete images go together with strong feelings. 'Metaphor', says Cecil Day Lewis, 'is the natural language of tension, or excitement', and we all know how, for example, a man who is angry readily finds all kinds of unpleasant images with which to describe his opponent. But the road of metaphor carries a two-way traffic, for not only does feeling issue in metaphor, but metaphor issues in feeling. Metaphorical language is always more alive, more vigorous, than language which is abstract. That is why there is such drive and force about some of the sayings of Samuel Rutherford. We are not being obscure if we say that Christ's love is infinite, but power is added to our expression of that truth if we say that His love 'hath neither brim nor bottom'. It is well enough to tell our congregations that they must expect the Christian life to be hard, but there will be much more vitality about our words if we say they must not expect to 'steal into Heaven with a full skin', or if we say, 'Our soft nature would have Heaven coming to our bedside when we are sleeping, and lying down with us that we might go to Heaven in warm clothes. But all that came found wet feet by the way, and sharp storms that did take the hide off their faces', or if we tell them quite simply, 'Men are not landed in Heaven sleeping'.

But similes and metaphors do much more than any of these things we have so far mentioned. They have a deep effect which is beyond their immediate purpose; they carry with them over-tones and implications which reveal more than the mere matter in hand. By relating that matter to other things, they give it a background and a setting, and enable our hearers to see it as part of a great whole.

Sometimes this effect is a very notable and obvious one. Take, for example, the beginning of the Collect of the First Sunday in Advent: 'Almighty God, give us grace that we may cast away the works of darkness, and put upon us the armour of light, now in the time of this mortal life, in which Thy Son Jesus Christ came to visit us in great humility.' There are several images here and they all deserve comment, but we must content ourselves with pointing to two of them. The phrase 'the works of darkness' refers to wrongdoing, but it also brings with it the ideas of night, fear, stealth, unseen powers, and hell. Similarly the word 'light' refers to goodness, but it also brings with it the ideas of safety, absence of concealment, healing, joy, the heavens above, and indeed heaven itself. The worshippers, using this collect, do not, of course, work all this out consciously, but it nevertheless forms an unconscious background in their minds, and they pray, not as isolated units, but as Christian men set in the midst of God's universe and inseparably related to it; Christianity is felt to be an essential part of the created order which God has ordained.

Not all our metaphors have so strong and clear an effect as this, but they all imply a universe in which things are related together, in which the laws found in one part govern also the rest, and (when they are used in a Christian context) in which all things are relevant to the faith. We remember once reading a popular exposition of a certain part of the Christian faith in which the author happened to have drawn his examples from many aspects of life—science, literature, art, sport, natural beauty, business life, and many more. The result was not merely that we were interested and illuminated; it was that we saw the Christian life as part of the great whole which is creation, and felt that all things were fashioned and upheld and moved by the hand of God; Christians seemed no longer to be a small minority in alien surroundings; they were an integral part of the cosmos, and that cosmos was so fashioned as to provide the right sort of environment for them in their task of learning how to live as children of God; nothing was irrelevant to the Kingdom of Heaven, but rather the whole earth was bright with God's glory. The author of the book did not say any of this at all; he was concerned with other aspects of the faith altogether. Nevertheless, he conveyed it by his imagery.

If the use of concrete images can serve us in so many ways, it is clear that we ought to make full use of them. There is no doubt that they come much more easily to some than to others; some people find it natural to think in pictures, whereas others have got used to thinking and talking in abstractions. But the world of the concrete image is not really strange to any of us. We all lived in it when we were children, and we still live there in our dreams. We can live in it also in our preaching, if we will take the trouble. All that is needed is for us to ask of every abstract statement and idea in our sermons the question which Jesus, who was so complete a Master of that world, used to ask in the days of His flesh about the Kingdom of God: 'Whereunto shall I liken it, or with what comparison shall I set it forth?'

PART TWO

Some Special Responsibilities

1. Preaching to Youth

By the REV. LEONARD P. BARNETT, B.D.

'WHY,' asked the pert young thing of the youth leader, 'when you say religion is dynamite, does Mr Dymm make it sound like sawdust?'

A fair, if somewhat shattering, question, for Brother Dymm. Because there's no doubt whatever about it, multitudes of perplexed and understandably (though almost always politely) scornful young people, *do* think that preaching is a dry-as-dust enterprise, high up on their list of things, real or imaginary, which Bore One Stiff. Look at any of the carefully documented Youth and Sunday School reports which have been so painstakingly assembled by several Churches since the war, on Why We Lost Them, or some allied theme. 'I was bored.' 'I lost interest.' 'It was the same old thing all the time.' As if we couldn't have guessed, remembering our own Sunday School days, and the tedious dissertations to which not infrequently we had to listen, either from the pulpit or from the big desk at which the Superintendent stood. The reason, basically, why teenagers are kittle cattle when it comes to rounding them up in the chapel corral, is precisely the same as applies to their elders. They've received the impression, from diverse sources, including the finished article itself, that sermons, for the most part, aren't really worth the time you have to spend listening to them.

'Caution,' said the wall notice by the telephone, 'Be sure Brain is engaged before Mouth is put into gear.' Nicely put. How terribly difficult, though; especially if at the receiving end there is a group of uninhibited and uncompromising young people!

Yet it can be done. Not, to be sure, by everybody. Not even, I believe, by nearly as many people as are pledged to try. But that's another story. Speaking for Christ, and to youth for Christ, irresistibly calls to mind the rather waspish remark of the great Doctor Johnson on the subject, forgive me, of women preaching. This phenomenon reminded the doctor of dogs that are taught to walk upon their hind legs. The marvel, he unkindly observed, was not that it was done badly; but that it was done at all. So with the task of preaching effectively to youth. It isn't easy.

Many an earnest brother, dismally aware of having failed to remove the glaze of boredom from the eyes of the youthful section of his congregation, must have wondered whether or not there was not some racy recipe to meet this situation. Perhaps you too are secretly aware of depressing failure. If so, let me say two things straight away. First you will find no such panacea in this article. Second, I beg leave to sit where you sit. We are all L-plate apprentices still, in this delicate and difficult craft of 'delivering the goods' to youth from Christian pulpits.

All the same, most of us must have ideas to share, which may contain some germ of truth to help us do a better job. I have but one; but under it can be grouped a few others stemming from it. All of them have one purely alphabetical likeness. They start with an 'I'. Indeed if you want a quick summary of what this article now sets out to describe, you could call it the 'Five-I Pattern'.

At the outset let us be clear about one thing. Although inevitably we must deal with aspects of Gospel truth in this article, it is *not* primarily about the stuff of the Gospel, *not* about theology, *not* about worship. It is plainly and simply about the art of 'getting it across'. It is about preaching technique; nothing less, but nothing more. I am taking it for granted that you are dedicated and evangelical, joyous, keen, intelligent and teachable, and that you are theologically and biblically well grounded and equipped as a would-be preacher of the Gospel. If you don't answer to that description, you are at least striving hard after it! Nobody else ought ever to get beyond the 'On Note' stage.

That being so, we can perhaps let the one and only idea loose, startlingly commonplace as it is bound to be.

I believe that, given the proper Christian qualifications of heart and mind, the one further all-embracing principle which will lead a preacher to the heart of whatever secret exists for capturing the attention and sympathy of young hearers, is very simply bound up in the one golden word . . . INTEREST!

And what, pray, does that mean? This: that at every stage, from first to last, the preacher who is out to 'get it across' to teenagers, must ask, ask, and ask again: 'Is this going to hold their interest? *Is it?*' This one sentence, asked and subsequently agonized over, is a major clue to the problem we are probing in this article. How often do we really stop to ask ourselves this question. I am not saying that this principle of 'Interest' must dominate and control the theme a preacher selects. Nor am I suggesting that topicality is the key to the solution, that nothing is admissible unless it immediately and quickly rings a bell within modern teenage environment and experience. Nothing should dominate the selection of a preacher's theme save the leading of the Holy Spirit. The fact is that one often has the most exhilarating and rewarding times preaching to youth *not* about topical themes such as 'Christianity and Road Safety' or 'The Sermon on the Mount and the H-Bomb', though these are very desirable themes, but on the basic and fundamental themes of Grace and Forgiveness, Mercy and Justice, the Incarnation and the Atonement, the Doctrine of Judgement, Heaven and Hell. All these, related of course to the contemporary situation. What other type of declaration of heavenly truth is of any earthly use?

What I am saying is that whatever is actually to be said by the preacher must square up to the insistent, imperative question, 'Is this going to hold them, going to engage their mind and imagination?'

If your experience in this matter is anything like mine, this must have meant many, so very many, hours of strenuous effort, patiently seeking after the right sort of presentation: the right sort of phrase: and the avoidance of the rolling platitude, the smooth cliché and well-worn jargon. Sometimes there comes the despairing feeling that this particular theme, this particular point, simply *couldn't* be made arresting by any means! At times that indeed has been the fact of the matter; and the sermon has been left on the stocks, maybe for good.

Yet such mental strife has also meant the golden reward—not always, but often enough to make it all worth while: that kind of deliverance which steers us away from the shoals of stodginess and out into the deeper waters where the fresh breezes of the Spirit blow. When *that* happens, even for the briefest spell, one senses the authentic and legitimate thrill of preaching the Gospel to youth so that they understand and appreciate, and respond with genuine interest. One other reward is yours, too; but that must keep to the end.

This golden principle, as I see it, affects the style, tenor, voice, language, length, and all else to do with the mode and manner of preaching. It clearly makes its impact from the very start of a sermon—with the Introduction. You have only got a strictly limited amount of time. Every word must count. There is no place for padding. In any case, padding always spells poverty. You must try to reach out and grasp their imagination in the first minute. A fearsome challenge. Can you meet it? Not always, of course. But try at least to avoid the trite, conventional, dull beginning. Once the teenage mind has resignedly said to itself, after the first minute, 'Oh dear, here we go again,' the preacher has loaded the scales heavily against himself.

Might that, do you think, be the reaction to this particular opening to a sermon?

My text for this evening is taken from the first book of Samuel, chapter 17, and verse 47: 'The battle is the Lord's.' Do you recall, I wonder, by whom the words were spoken? They come from the same chapter from which we read, earlier on in this service. There is scarcely a more enthralling narrative anywhere in the Old Testament—indeed in the whole of literature—than that which depicts the young man David courageously standing forth to meet the challenge of his formidable adversary, the giant warrior Goliath.

Can we enter, perhaps, into the feelings of David as he left the friendly protection of the Israelite lines, and went forward to encounter Goliath alone? If you know the chapter concerned, you will remember that before he was permitted to take the field against Goliath, David was obliged to face discouragement from his own side. His own brethren, in particular, were scornful—indeed angry—with him, for his presumption. 'Presumption', in fact, is the very word which the Revised Standard Version attributes to Eliab, David's eldest brother, as he accused the younger lad of leaving the sheep, in untrustworthy fashion, in order to enjoy the more exciting spectacle of a battle.

But David was not discouraged! No indeed! He persisted in his determination to enter the lists and bring Goliath low. He finds that the King himself, the redoubtable Saul, has sent for him. And at first he most respectfully accepts the direction of his monarch, and allows himself to be equipped with his cumbersome armour. But he finds his customary freedom of movement virtually impossible. It is only then that he seems to take matters into his own hands, and goes forth with only his tried and trusted staff and sling to aid him.

And so it is that at the time to which our text relates, we find the mighty Goliath face to face with the puny David. The challenge has been thrown down, and David is taking it up. But he goes forward to his time of testing with one great thought uppermost in his mind. It is not for his own personal aggrandisement or renown that he ventures forth against Goliath. He is marching forward against the enemy of God. And so he puts into words the thought which buoys him up and invests him with far more courage than his brethren. 'The battle,' he asserts, 'is the Lord's.'

Could a preacher be expected, deliberately bearing in mind the teenage section of his congregtaion, to contrive something rather more geared to their particular mind and outlook? I think so. What about this?

Do you remember the popular radio programme 'Who said That?' A panel of experts who seemed to know what everybody had ever said to anyone, tried to identify well-known quotations—including some from the Bible. Here's one they might have used. Let's try it ourselves. This is it: 'The Battle is the Lord's.' Who said that? 'The Battle is the Lord's!' It's our text for tonight—I Samuel 17⁴⁷. It wasn't whispered. It wasn't said by somebody who was whistling to keep his courage up. It came at the end of a shouting match, just before the big fight started. You could almost say it was the cue for action. And what action!

It was said by a little fellow to a very big one. They were scared to death of the big fellow. He stood nine foot six in his socks, and his coat of mail alone weighed well over a couple of hundred pounds. He was a killer. No wonder he put the fear of death into the other side. That is, until the little fellow came along.

Well, you've guessed already, of course, especially if you were quick enough to notice that the chapter the text comes from is the same chapter we were reading from a few minutes back. 'The Battle is the Lord's'— David said it. Not cockily, mind. This wasn't a case of a silly young fool rushing in where sensible angels feared to tread. He shouted it with all the certainty of a man who knew he was on the winning side. He had good reason to think it. He was lightly clad. He could run fast. Goliath couldn't. Goliath was a sitting target; a dead duck before he started, if he had but known it. David was a crack shot. That unprotected forehead of Goliath was simply asking for one between the eyes; and David was as good with his sling as those crack shots we read about elsewhere in the Old Testament. Listen to this verse from Judges 20, where they're talking about the Israelite Army. Among them were (I'm reading from verse 16 now) 'seven hundred picked men who were left-handed; every one could sling a stone at a hair, and not miss'. There's accuracy for you! David was as good as that; and he knew it. What's more, even if the first stone missed, he had four more. He wouldn't have chosen five if he knew perfectly well he hadn't a ghost of a chance of using more than one. On the contrary, he knew perfectly well that he *would* have a chance. But it wasn't necessary.

All the same, accidents do happen. And this wasn't a phoney sort of fight. It wasn't played out, like so many we look at from time to time, under the blazing arc-lamps of a film or television studio, with the make-up man waiting in the wings to apply the artificial cuts and bruises, quite painlessly. This was real life. This was a genuine fight to a finish. One man was to die, the other to triumph. Until it actually happened, nobody could say for sure which.

So watch him now, this fresh-faced youngster, with his calm, sensible confidence, playing it cool in the presence of this brassy man-mountain, Goliath, clanking forward like a human tank. Here he comes, mad with rage, bellowing his fearsome curses. How dare these dogs of Israel offer him, a champion of champions, such an insult! He, Goliath, to fight with a miserable beardless boy!

But listen to David, giving as good as he gets. 'You come to me with a sword and a spear and a javelin!' he cries. 'But I come to you in the name of the Lord of Hosts! This day the Lord will deliver you into my hand, that all this assembly may know that the Lord saves not with sword and spear . . . for the battle is the Lord's!'

Any good? Did it make you wince now and then? 'Dead duck', 'crack shot', . . . 'killer', . . . 'ghost of a chance', 'make-up man', . . . 'playing it cool'. Such language wouldn't come naturally to you? Too crude? This is fair comment. I'm not for a moment suggesting this is the one and only treatment for this theme, this text. Far from it. I offer it simply as the *sort* of brisk and contemporary style which stands a far better chance of *holding interest* for the teenager—and so permitting the preacher to forge ahead with his theme, having—we hope—scored an initial advantage, an all-important one.

Within this sort of introduction, and indeed throughout every sermon beamed on teenage wavelengths, I believe there should be apparent another 'I' which it's worth looking at with care— 'I' for 'Immediacy'. The aim above was, in part, to bring the scene to life; so to dramatize it from the Old Testament that the characters got up from the printed page to walk up and down before the inner eye of the congregation. In short, the idea was to make the subject live. Nothing new here, of course. Every reputable discussion on homiletics heavily underlines the same precise point. But how many preachers take it to heart?

Let's try again to focus on the difference between the conventional but all too often tedious kind of presentation, and the presentation behind which lies an honest effort to *see* what is being said, through the mind of a teenager. He thinks, as most people do, in terms of pictures rather than in abstract ideas or catalogues of facts. Here is a short excerpt from a sermon during Christian Aid Week (text, Luke 10^{37}, *NEB*. 'Go and do as he did').

First, what we might venture to call the factual treatment.

In the Near East, at the present time, one of the more interesting features of Inter-Church Aid—this time sponsored by the Church of Scotland—is the gift of a large consignment of cloth woven in Scotland, which is being used in Jordan by young Arab refugees, of both sexes, who are being trained in dress-making and tailoring. From the Arab refugee camps annually some 30,000 young people come to maturity, with little prospect of employment. How good it is to think that through the spirit of the Good Samaritan, working in the hearts of Scottish Christians, thousands of non-Christians, fellow-citizens of the world nevertheless, are being given a real chance in life.

Well, there you are. Clear, factual, authentic, telling its own story. But likely to hold teenage imagination and interest? Or would something like this be nearer the mark?

I want you to come with me for a moment to a rather odd place—a mill, up in Scotland. They weave and store cloth there. Look over in that corner—bale after bale of cloth, scores of them, piled high. Every one has 'Jordan—Near East Christian Council' stamped on it. It won't be left there long. That cloth is wanted—urgently. Let's follow it on its way to the eastern end of the Mediterranean. It's on its way to training centres run by people from the YMCA and YWCA. If you were to take a look inside, you'd see crowds of fellows and girls—remarkably like some of us, apart from their slightly darker colouring. Where have they come from? They've come from refugee camps. They were born in those camps. They've been homeless all their lives. Now they're teenagers. They've never known what it was like to have a home, with ordinary comforts and amenities—like clean running water, a decent bed, three square meals a day. All they've known is the discomfort and squalor of life in tents and shacks, all weathers; with little food and less money. A bare, comfortless existence. Thirty thousand of these people become teenagers every year. Thirty thousand, think of it! And next to none of them find any sort of a job. Next to none are able to learn any sort of skill or craft. Anybody doing anything about it? Yes, indeed! This is where our bales of cloth come into the picture. Christian people are trying to use both grace and gumption, like the Good Samaritan did. That cloth is being used to train those young people to become dressmakers and tailors, so that wherever they may travel in the years to come, they will have a skill in their fingers. They'll be able to earn their own living. Would you like to be dependent on other people's charity all your days? No, and neither do these young people. So Christians are at work, caring, giving, sending, organizing and training, trying to heal the hidden wounds of resentment and despair, apathy and hopelessness.

Who paid for the cloth? Scottish Christians. Who is at work helping to train these young people, to give them life and hope? Other Christian people! What makes the whole thing gloriously possible in the first place? Christian partnership! You're in it! I'm in it! And millions like us. Right round the globe the network of strategic Christian co-operation spreads ever more strongly. Thank God for it!

Is there not a note of immediacy here, which is lacking from the first, rather trite and lack-lustre recital of the facts? Isn't this way of presenting the same material something which anybody with a will to win could achieve? It is, I believe, a technique which, if its merits are agreed, can be learned and practised by most men and women. Part of the technique, for instance, is the judicious use of the present tense. Another, short pithy sentences. Another, the deliberate rejection of the effort to deliver a sermon comprised of complete sentences with faultless syntax and grammar. Nothing should deliberately break the rules of syntax and grammar, however. We are emphatically not pleading for slovenly English, still less for horrible gaffes and plain error. I suppose the style might roughly be described as 'ejaculatory'; though the word sounds a bit pretentious. 'Dramatic'—would that do? There is nothing wrong with dramatization—our Lord used it often enough! There's a world of difference between drama and theatricality (if such a word exists!). The one is legitimate and indeed, as I see it, utterly vital. The other is an offensive hindrance. The one adds colour and life; the other, mere glamour and titillation of an unwelcome kind.

All kinds of angles and facets, bits and pieces belonging to the world of popular entertainment are, of course, potentially useful to the preacher who wants to reach out and enter into the world of immediate teenage experience. When the popular musical *My Fair Lady* was enjoying its first triumphant months at Drury Lane, and the catchy melodies were upon most teenage lips, I took four of the titles as themes for sermons on some basic aspects of Christian truth: *Wouldn't it Be Loverly* (The Kingdom of God); *With a Little Bit of Luck* (Authentic Religion and Humbug); *Show Me!* ('If Thou be the Son of God come down from the Cross. . . .' Demonstrable Christianity); and a *Hymn to him* (The Natural man—and the Man in Christ). The sermons began where the young people were and attempted to lead them to where God wanted them to be. The opposite technique, which the late Dr Macalister Brew used to pillory so rightly, is to attempt to take young people from where they are not, to where they have not the slightest desire to be.

Let's move on to the third 'I'—'Imagination'. Rare quality! But supplies could be improved I believe. It's *time* we perhaps need to give ourselves, as much as anything. Imagination needs to be wooed. And successful wooing is hardly ever a rush job! Imagination, of course, has been implied right from the start of this article, and must be, to the end. The five strands of this 'I' pattern are all interwoven. We are only drawing the strands apart for convenience' sake.

But let us think now about imagination. If it was our Lord's superb imagination which led Him to devise such matchless stories that we in our day can make them live in the hearing of men of very different culture and environment, is it too much to expect that we too, in our own small way, could devise imaginatively our own ways of imprinting eternal truth upon the minds of teenage listeners, using contemporary parables? (That incidentally, was an intolerably long and involved sentence, which no self-respecting preacher to youth would ever employ!)

Even if we cannot ourselves think of such parables, they may be quarried from the sources others have left us. Take Major Lewis Hastings's African travel book, for instance, *Dragons are Extra.* (The explanation of the title itself, by the way, affords yet another example of modern parable.) In that book is described the way in which, deep in the heart of the jungle, Hastings came across piles of sticks carefully and improbably piled in rough forest-fire fashion. What was the explanation? At last it dawned. Chimpanzees! Hastings goes on to imagine them recollecting the way they had seen humans arrange such sticks. This they do. Then, having completed their imitative task they squat back on their haunches waiting for the miracle of smoke and flame—a miracle which obstinately refused to materialize. They had learned the mechanics of the business, but they did not know the secret of fire. All was ready save the vital spark. And without it, their patient labour was in vain.

Who needs to have the parable expounded? 'O Thou who camest from above, the pure, celestial fire to impart! . . .' So many glossy new houses with human beings inside them, waiting for the pure flame of love to turn them into homes; so many blue prints for the New Jerusalem waiting for the spark of grace to kindle them into life and reality! So many . . . but who could not go on?

But there are more parables which are waiting to be told, and which patient meditation, fertilized and nourished by constant reading, listening and looking, may succeed in recognizing. Here are two such which even if they fail to commend themselves to the reader, may encourage him to make better discoveries of his own. They are certainly waiting to be made.

First, an extract from a sermon seeking to bring home to the youthful congregation an awareness of the certainty of death, and at the same time, something of the shallowness of modern man in his attitude to it.

Life is like a steady flowing river, calm and clear, and thronged with people, each paddling his own little canoe downstream. Some paddle for dear life. Some take it easy. Some simply drift idly along. All except a tiny few keep close to their fellows, travelling deliberately with them. The banks of the river on each side, as far as the eye can see, are crammed with interest. There's something to occupy you all the time; never a dull moment, save for those who won't look. It is, on the whole, an absorbing, fascinating journey. The only thing is, it's quite clear the journey has an end. What's more, nobody can quite see what *is* going to happen. All they *can* see is that finally the river winds its way into a vast dark cavern set in a far-off mountain-side. There are so many delightful bends and twists in the river however, that apart from the odd submerged snags which may wreck a canoe here and there—to the sorrow of those round about—the vast majority of people can confidently expect a long and engrossing journey before the nearness of the end of the journey really begins to impress itself uncomfortably upon them.

All the same, they know it's there. Away ahead the cavern is dark and huge. They can't fool themselves that it's an illusory trick of the light. It's as real as the frail craft they're travelling in. And, sometimes, they are afraid, because the cavern looks so black, so impenetrable, so menacing. A few fellow-travellers talk about it being an entrance to an even more splendid journey, but this seems like idle talk. Nobody's ever come back upstream bringing any real evidence that the notion's sound—though again *some* travellers insist that they have an unseen Companion on the journey who did just that. Most people, however, think these are rather odd folk who are kidding themselves and imagine all that sort of thing, whistling to keep their courage up. Hardly anybody ever speaks about that dark cavern in the distance—and there's so much to look at, and talk about, on the nearest bank. But the thought hovers about on the threshold of their minds, sometimes distressingly persistent. And they wonder. . . .

You may possibly feel this is simply a detailed simile rather than a parable proper. Terminology matters little. What matters much is the achievement of the aim—to remind the hearers that time is—after all—an ever-rolling stream, and that it matters greatly how we travel, and where we are convinced that the stream is leading us, and why.

On a totally different theme, here is another sort of parable (if the word be allowed), in a modern idiom and setting, this time seeking to bring to life one of the basic ideas of the gospel—forgiveness.

The aim is to show why, if God's design for human living is to be achieved, the way of endless readiness to forgive, is for Him, the *only* way.

Most of us, at one time or another, have taken part in a play. Right. Let's imagine that's just what is happening. Here is the producer with his play. He has read it, studied it, soaked himself in it, as you might say. It's a magnificent play. It has something to say. No silly, sloppy, thin stuff—this is first-rate drama, calling for the best possible talent. It's worth every ounce of effort anybody can give to it, from the producer to the man with only one line to say. It's an ambitious play, calling for a big cast, men, women, and younger people.

Then rehearsals start. The producer finds out he has chosen his cast with every good intention; but if you were he, you'd quickly start to think that these would-be players haven't got what it takes, or don't justify his faith in them. A few of them are willing to listen to him, in a fairly reasonable fashion, so long as he doesn't ask them to do anything too undignified or difficult. Others of them, chosen for the big parts, swiftly start showing all the symptoms of that deadly disease, swelled head. They hog the stage. They're jealous of the other leading players. Some of the bit players are jealous too—they think *they* were cut out for stardom too, if the producer had had the sense to recognize their talent.

There are still others who simply won't take the trouble to learn. They want the interest and excitement of being on the stage, but they're blessed if they're going in for the hard fag of learning their lines. They mumble and fluff their dialogue, and put other people off.

There's another group who think the whole thing is a first-class skylark. They haven't any real intention of getting down to the job, and treating it seriously. They fool about, they're never there when they're wanted, they're always making an uproar somewhere or other when the producer wants quietness. In fact they are just a thundering nuisance.

One thing in with another, you'd forgive the producer for chucking his hand in, and walking out on the lot of them.

That's one thing which he could do, simply, easily, and with every justification.

He could say, 'Look, you lot! We've got a great play here—a play tremendously well-worth doing. It could be the hit of the season. But if you aren't going to knuckle down to it, if you will persist in making this ghastly mess of it, then I'm through. You don't deserve to take part, and I'm certainly not going to bother my head about you!'

Or he could take a different line.

He could do the best job possible, with as many folk as were in earnest, and who wanted the play to go on. He'd have endless difficulties, but he *could try*. And as far as the rest were concerned, he could hang on, with unconquerable patience and unremitting good will, *waiting for them to come to their senses*. He could stay on call, as it were, until the jealous people, the skylark squad, the layabout lot, had come to realize what insufferable fools they were making of themselves, and how heavy a burden they were putting upon everyone else. He could stay ready for action, until the swelled heads had gone down, and the giggles were over, and everybody had got a sight of the play, splendid and glorious instead of a vision of their own name in neon lights, blotting out everything else. And the producer would be ready instantly, to forgive and forget, the moment they came to their senses.

Well now . . .

> . . . *all the world's a stage,*
> *And all the men and women* actually *players.* . . .

Beg pardon, Mr Shakespeare, but we'd like to amend your unforgettable line ever so slightly.

Listen! Here stands God Almighty, Maker of Heaven and Earth. He built the stage itself. He has the script in His hand—a magnificent piece, the drama of real life, patterned upon perfect Beauty, Truth and Goodness. He is Author and Producer. He has spoken and written, His true and lively Word. In fact, in a manner of speaking, He also stands ready to take the leading part, and to show the players how. He is never off the stage.

What a drama He has planned! It is the prototype of every piece you ever saw on the tiny platforms of earth. It is the story of the everlasting battle of right with wrong, light with darkness, truth with falsehood; its aim and intention is the triumph of goodness and love, the sweeping away of everything that hurts and destroys and makes for a lie—the drying of tears once and for all—the building of a city all light and health and joy, in which the inhabitants serve the Builder and Maker, their King and their Father, day and night.

But how stupid these would-be players are! They think that the play revolves around *them*! There's no end to their vanity, their cussedness, their itch for the limelight.

And still God stands, ready and willing to take up the threads of His work, from wherever human sin breaks it off. What is more, He does not just stand waiting, motionless, inactive, until we begin to take an interest in Him. Looking at Him from one point of view, we see that He is not standing. He is hanging from a cross.— In its light, we see what our pride and prejudice, our envy and spite, do to His Father-heart. We look again and we see nail-imprinted hands, outstretched to welcome us back into His goodly company. He is ready not only to show us where to stand, and what to do, but to stand by us, so that we can take our cue from Him, now and always.

It is happening all the time, everywhere.

And so to the last of the five 'I's.

Some years ago, a pert and most attractive young woman, who was frequently taken out by various young gentlemen—but seldom taken in—told me, with much amusement, of an evening spent in the company of a robust and extrovert American. He had talked with dynamic energy for the best part of three to four hours, stopping in midflight every now and then to demand, staccato fashion, 'Get the pikchrr, honey?'

Whenever we preach to youth, our aim must be to help them to 'get the picture'—sharply, clearly, compellingly etched upon their minds. In a word we must *illustrate*. In a sense, throughout this article, I have been trying continuously to demonstrate this very point. Almost everything offered above is by way of illustration of the points at issue. It seemed the only sensible way, to offer tangible examples of the kind of thing that I believe is needed. If they pass muster, well and good. If not, they should at least stimulate criticism. Go then and do better!

One—fairly obvious—word about 'illustrations for youth'. They need not always be *about* youth or childhood, but they ought not to be so remote from the field of their experience and imagination as to be divested of life and reality. They should be drawn from their world, as far as possible, and be about things with which they are familiar.

In this regard every daily paper—especially the more popular press—and almost every magazine will yield grist for the mill.

Teenagers are news—often unhappily, not infrequently heart-warmingly. Never a week passes but what some idea of human interest, featuring a youngster somewhere or other, makes the headlines—even if only on the inside pages.

Here is the sort of thing I mean. Some time ago, four teenagers walking back home to an outlying village from a Saturday night dance, approached a level crossing. They heard a train in the distance. High spirits and recklessness prompted one of the boys to suggest a dare—'Last across'. The two girls were sensibly scared and scuttled to safety, with one of the boys. The last they ever heard of the fourth boy was his derisive cry 'You're chicken!' as the engine thundered up. The next moment the buffers caught him and hurled him to his death. Here is the kind of contemporary tragedy—commonplace, alas, yet full of drama—which can make an effective impact upon the mind of a modern teenager.

The contemporary scene, however, affords equally good and effective material. There is, for instance, the Fontana paperback *Dying We Live*, edited by Trevor Huddlestone; and the same author's *Naught for Your Comfort*; there is our own Colin Morris's *The Hour Past Midnight*, and a whole stream of other similar books chronicling the agony and deep Christian challenge of our time. They offer an abundance of illustration which is as relevant as it is gripping.

Out of this wealth take for instance the opening page of Richard Solberg's *God and Caesar in East Germany* (expensive, I know, but I got my local library to buy the copy I read!) in which he tells the story of young Hansi Wendler, East German Pastor's daughter, a teacher in training, interviewed by her college principal and the local political commissar about her S.C.M. membership. She faced a direct demand to relinquish her Christian associations, she steadfastly refused. As she came out from the fateful interview, she encountered a strident poster on the wall opposite. An enormous Karl Marx, surrounded by a crowd of eager young students, confronted a Cross, and a Bible. The caption beneath read: 'This we will not tolerate!' The grim sequel was the expulsion of Hansi and ten other Christian students, and an end to their hopes of a dedicated teaching career. But was all lost, and this witness without point? Or did Hansi win a victory that day, for God and His Kingdom?

On a very different plane: what of humour as an ally in illustrating, in this task of making Christian truth clear to teenagers? A tricky tool to use indeed; nothing ponderous, longwinded, 'corny', at any cost! But given the time and opportunity, the tool can be invaluable. Real humour, if we take the greatest care that the bounds of good taste are never for a moment crossed, can be of enormous help in getting close to young people and enlisting their good will and sympathy.

It may not be out of place to refer to something from a book in which I once attempted to set down the principles of sound Church Youth Club leadership. I called the idea the 'Doctrine of the First-rate'. What I then said, applies, I believe, as much to preaching to youth, as to guiding them within the club community.

Every self-respecting church club leader should believe strongly in the 'Doctrine of the First-rate'. . . . Do your bit towards replacing the old-established tradition that because a job is voluntary, it must therefore be treated as less binding, less demanding, than the job for which you get a reward, and hopes of promotion for outstanding performance. We often assert our duty to give no less than the best to God. . . . Let us see that in terms of . . . being ready to attend conscientiously to the trivial bits and pieces of which it is all composed. . . . Genius is an infinite capacity for taking pains. How utterly true of club work is that old adage! How many leaders are tempted, at times, to bemoan their lack of striking qualities when all the while, if they will patiently do the job that's nearest, followed by the thing next to that, they would be on the way to achieving grand results. Success in club work is *not* first a matter of being blessed with the radiant, captivating personality, the attractive personal charm, the ability to do a parlour trick or two. It can and will be achieved by the man or woman of no outstanding endowment of personality, but who is a person of good will and Christian experience, ready to see that in careful attention to tiny pettifogging detail lies the most significant clue to effective leadership.

If you will be good enough to transpose that paragraph, as it were, so that *preaching* and not leadership is the theme, it fairly represents what I firmly believe about the task of preaching to youth. 'The trivial bits and pieces . . . tiny pettifogging detail . . .' these are the elements which together characterize the true craftsman in the skilled task of opening the gates of life in Christ, to today's teenagers. They demand and deserve our best efforts— the best efforts of men and women who believe in a doctrine daringly entitled 'Christian Perfection'. And we believe too that the Holy Spirit can make ordinary advocates into ambassadors extraordinary, speaking boldly and effectively, as they ought to speak.

Yet there is, of course, a price that we must be willing to pay: that extra ten minutes spent searching through all kinds of reading matter, in quest for source material which might ring a bell with young people; the odd half-hour spent viewing and listening to programmes which give an insight into the likes and dislikes of young people, their hopes and fears, prejudices and pleasures—however much the preacher may sometimes shudder, perhaps, at their taste; the deliberate attempt to spend time in the company of modern teenagers (when last did you spend an hour in a steadfast resolve to try to understand and appreciate young people and to 'get their wavelength'?)—all these are marks of someone who really yearns to speak effectively to youth, for the Master whom they are unconsciously seeking.

It is time, finally, for me to redeem a promise made above, regarding the 'one other reward' which I was bold enough to guarantee to those who are learning the satisfaction and joy of preaching effectively to youth.

Some years ago, I interviewed a modern prince of the pulpit whose name is a household word for attractive, intelligible, relevant preaching. 'Please could you tell me,' I asked, 'how you visualize the task of preaching? What is your recipe for an effective sermon?' I shall never forget his reply. It has profoundly influenced my own approach to preaching, and I hope it always will. 'I always beam my sermons,' he said, 'at the head of an intelligent fifteen-year-old.' Then he went on. 'Your intelligent fifteen-year-old,' he said, 'is just about as intelligent at that age as he is ever likely to be. All that is lacking is the experience and maturity of judgement which time alone can bring. I therefore believe that if I can be intelligible and interesting to an intelligent fifteen-year-old, I shall have made the best possible use of my preaching time. If I aim deliberately to say things which only age and maturity permit my hearers to understand, I shall bore my youthful listeners, and I may be a positive hindrance to them in their quest after Christian truth. So, as I prepare my sermons, I am always asking myself: "How is this going to sound to a teenager?"'

Multitudes of people believe the speaker to have been the greatest preacher of his age. We do well to listen to him. I believe his logic, and his conclusions, are irresistible. Not just sometimes but always, our preaching should be submitted to the same test: 'How is this going to sound to a teenager?'

2. The Preacher as Christian Citizen

By the REV. KENNETH G. GREET

AN irate letter from a preacher arrived one morning in the Department of Christian Citizenship of the Methodist Church. It began with the ominous words 'Dear Friend', and continued: 'Last year was World Refugee Year, the year before was World Mental Health Year, and this is Road Safety Year. Kindly tell me (*a*) what year it is next year, and (*b*) when I shall get the chance to preach the gospel.'

A reply was sent by return. It read: 'Dear Friend, The answer to your enquiry is (*a*) Next year is Christian Home and Family Year; (*b*) You have fifty-two Sundays a year on which to preach the gospel.'

This brief correspondence really takes us to the heart of several most important questions. Is it possible to preach the gospel at all save in a quite specific context? Can the preaching of the gospel ever be regarded as an end in itself? What is Christian preaching?

In this article we shall examine these among other questions and, as a clue to the sort of answer which will be provided, let us look at an exciting and moving book by Colin Morris called *The Hour after Midnight*. It tells the story of what happened when a young minister went out to preach the gospel in Northern Rhodesia. For a time his ministry was outwardly successful. Congregations increased. He dealt with biblical themes and was regarded as an impressive and gifted preacher. But he was troubled in conscience because he had not dealt with the burning issue of race relations. He knew that to deal with this explosive subject from the pulpit would cause offence, and that there were those who argued that the pulpit should not become involved in the discussion of political matters. But could a preacher claim that his message was relevant if he remained silent on the most pressing problem of the day? He announced that he would preach a series of sermons on the Christian approach to race relations.

Those who are tempted to think that the claim that the Bible is dynamite is merely rhetorical exaggeration should note carefully what happened to Colin Morris. During the first sermon members of the congregation marched out in protest. They made sure that the doors slammed behind them. The large congregation dwindled. The preacher had gone too far. Religion was all right as long as it was kept in its place.

Was this particular preacher right? Or, to put the question in more general terms, ought we to keep our Christian citizenship and our preaching separate—except, of course, on the third Sunday in November, when we are officially exhorted to bring them together, and when those who object can stay at home? In various ways we are probably all tempted to make this dichotomy. It may help us to see that it is false and unscriptural if we examine four statements sometimes made by those who tend to divorce preaching from the swirl and rush of contemporary events. Such examination cannot but assist us to see more clearly the task of the preacher as Christian Citizen.

THE WORD OF GOD AND THE WORDS OF MEN

Some preachers claim that their concern is with the Word of God rather than the words of men.

This point of view represents a misunderstanding of a fundamental truth. The fact is that the Bible consists of the words of men. The half-baked notion that the Bible descended from heaven is a mockery, and completely unrelated to the actual mechanics of mediation. It is as ridiculous as the screen version of how the Ten Commandments were written on the tables of stone.

We cannot too often remind ourselves that the God who speaks through the Bible is One who borrows the voices of men. It is no service to truth to try to obscure this fact and all that it implies. On the contrary, our understanding of truth is very much dependent upon our grasping the necessity of sound scholarship and accurate translation. For to say that God uses human language is to assert that He has chosen to employ a highly flexible medium. Words not only change their meaning, they sometimes actually get lost. At least two things, therefore, are involved in the task of translation. One is the compiling of as accurate a text as possible. The other is the attempt to understand not only what a man said but what, in terms of our present language and thought-forms, he meant. Even when this has been done we have to reckon with the imperfection of the instruments God chose to be His spokesmen, and with our own lack of perception and the prejudice which hinders our understanding.

It is apparent that any claim that the preacher is concerned with the Word of God and not with the words of men is insupportable. It is as foolish as the boast of an aircraft designer that he is not in the least interested in gravity but only in keeping his plane in the sky. The end of such ignorance would be disaster. Any preacher who does not care deeply about words, who has not a deep respect for language, begins with an initial disability which must surely be fatal to his effectiveness as a prophet. Because often much is expected from us it is natural that we should sometimes grow tired of the sound of our own voices. But we must never allow weariness to cause us to doubt the value of speech. 'What's the good of talking?' is a misguided complaint. The God whom we worship is a God who speaks. If words are important to Him we ought not to complain at the discipline of making ourselves masters of the art of language.

It is a divinely appointed fact that the Word of God comes through the word of man. Language is the gift of God to the preacher. Out of a vast heap of words we are free to select and arrange. The result can be a dull discourse which drifts aimlessly from an uncertain start to an inconclusive end. Or it can be a message which by its very lucidity and logical orderliness inspires men to action and high resolve. God will not despise those who, in humility, offer Him the best speech of which they are capable in the conviction that He can and will turn human words into Divine Communication.

Here, then, is the first fact to be underlined: we must not make a false dichotomy between the word of God and the words of men. But this truth runs deeper still, as will be apparent if we turn to the second of our four points.

THE ETERNAL AND THE TEMPORAL

Some preachers claim that their concern is with the eternal rather than the temporal.

Occasionally when this claim is made one listens with deep sympathy. At a recent Ecumenical Conference, attended by Christian leaders from both sides of the Iron Curtain, a bearded priest from a Communist country described the situation in which he was involved. His church was not allowed what might be called extra-mural activities. He reported that often there was a representative of the State taking notes of his sermons. Any criticism of government policy was likely to lead to trouble. Flinging out his arms he said: 'All that is left to us is to preach the gospel.'

What, however, one wants to ask, does the phrase mean? For at the heart of the gospel is the sublime paradox that the eternal has broken through into time. Jesus was the Man who broke history in two. In order that God might be known by men He suffered Himself to be subject to the limitations of time and space. At the heart of the gospel is the Divine Incarnation, the fact of embodiment. The preacher of that gospel is, therefore, by its very nature, concerned about the temporal as well as the eternal, because the one is conveyed through the other. Christianity is first of all about what God has done. As St Paul said: 'I must make it clear to you, my friends that the gospel you heard me preach is no human invention' (Gal. 1^{11}, NEB).

If it is true that the Word of God comes through the words of men, it is also true that the revelation of God and His purposes comes through the processes of history. History is the workshop of God; time is the roaring loom on which the garment of His kingly rule is woven. This is why the preaching of the Bible is 'situational preaching'. The human situation is not something extraneous, for God is in every situation. In all the flow and flux of contemporary events the man of faith sees the Hand of God stretched out to judge and to save. It is this that imparts to the Old Testament narrative a grandeur and gives to it a distinctive quality. The Hebrews had no secular historians. History is not a secular business. If we sometimes talk as if it were, the rebuke of the prophets would be 'Your God is too Small'.

The incarnation of the Son of God is the logical culmination of the Divine purpose revealed in the Old Testament. The gospel is in very truth the fulfilment of all that the prophets wrote and spoke. The birth of Jesus is indeed a unique event but its uniqueness is that of the God who is both transcendent and immanent and who, all through the story, has revealed Himself paradoxically as the Eternal willing to imprison Himself within time, that we might escape from the limitations of the temporal and enjoy the glorious liberty of the Children of God.

The parables of Jesus are a vivid commentary upon the saving truth that we have been examining. They are, incidentally, rich with suggestiveness for the preacher. Not, mark you, that preachers have always handled them wisely. Parables can be dangerous ammunition in the hands of those who do not understand what they are and why they are. They are not allegories, stories concocted, like children's addresses, to drive home a moral or two. Rather, they are observations from real life. They require no moralistic embroidering for they contain their own truth. The reason why they contain their own truth is that at the heart of every situation there is God. So Jesus catches a fleeting moment of time and holds it up as the mirror of eternity.

This, then, is the second fact to be underlined: we must not make a false dichotomy between the eternal and the temporal. This truth carries us on to some very practical conclusions, as we shall see if we turn to our third and fourth points.

THE SPIRITUAL AND THE MATERIAL

Some preachers claim that their concern is with the spiritual rather than the material.

In fact, of course, however well-intentioned the protagonists of this view may be, we are dealing with one of the most persistent of all heresies. The paradox of God's plan of revelation and redemption is not exhausted by the statements that the Word of God comes through the words of Men, and that the Eternal is made known through the temporal. It is part of the same truth that the material is the medium of the spiritual. No part of the assertion of Christian faith has been more fiercely assailed than this. All heresy results from the inability or unwillingness of men to hold together what God has joined. The very earliest Christian heresies were rooted in a denial of the truth that God makes the material the vehicle of the spiritual.

This particular kind of heresy did not, of course, come in with Christianity. It has a much longer history. The particular form of it which affected early Christian thought was known as Gnosticism. At the heart of the complex of beliefs to which this name was attached lay the dualistic notion that creation was not one and undivided but that matter and spirit were at war with one another. The material world was evil and the road of salvation, therefore, was envisaged as a pathway of escape. Alexander the Great carried the benefits of Greek culture to the lands of the Orient, but the Eastern religious contributed powerfully to the later period of Greek civilization. This oriental dualism left an indelible mark on Hellenistic culture, and, therefore, on the thinking of the Christian Church.

No one can measure the extent of the influence of this alien dualism upon the course of Christian history. The naturalism of the Hebrew people who rejoiced in the wonders of God's material Creation, and saw in the beauties of nature the hem of the Divine garment, is in some measure replaced by a morbid fear and suspicion of the material world. The human body in particular is looked upon as a tomb, from which the soul must desire to escape in order to find redemption. To recall this disastrous departure from the truth is not just to make a point of academic interest or to take an excursion into a long-buried past. The lurking belief that the material world is evil, and that the body, and its sexual functions in particular, are tainted, still works great mischief. Christians often seem ill at ease when discussing the significance of the material. It is, apparently, easier to talk about 'spiritual things', though the conjunction of these two words is full of interest and suggests that we don't really know what we are talking about.

We can only escape from damaging confusion by accepting the full Christian doctrine of creation. At the centre of the Christian gospel is the fact of Incarnation, the sacramental truth that God was in Christ. He who created a world to show forth His glory, was Himself made Man. In that flesh we see Him who is Spirit and Truth; His voice is the voice that rolls the stars along.

To move swiftly from the sublime to the searching: we had better stop trying to be more spiritual than God. It is excitingly significant that of the three great movements making for renewal in the life of the modern Church two are directly concerned with the rediscovery of the importance of the material. Biblical theology is stressing the centrality of the doctrine of the Incarnation, and the search for a better biblical text (and notably the publication of the first part of the New English Bible) has aroused much popular interest in the mechanics of translation and interpretation. The liturgical movement has resulted in a new emphasis on the place of Holy Communion in the life and worship of the Christian congregation. Here at the central observance of our religion our faith is earthed: the holy symbols are manufactured articles, bread and wine, the fruit of the labour of God and man. It may be added that one of the major results of the third great movement of renewal, which we call ecumenical, is that the hungry are being more efficiently fed and diseased bodies healed. Thus love is made meaningful because compassion becomes concrete.

Clearly, then, the third fact to be underlined is this: we must not make a false dichotomy between the eternal and the temporal. One further point remains.

THE PERSONAL AND THE SOCIAL

Some preachers claim that their concern is with the personal rather than with the social.

This attitude is sometimes the result of too exclusive and limited a view of one aspect of the teaching of the Bible. The apostles of apocalypse represent that view in its most exaggerated form. They believe that the end of the world is at hand, and that therefore the preacher must concentrate on preparing the souls of men for the great spiritual encounter with the returning Saviour. Any attempt to come to grips with the pressing social, political and economic problems of the day is regarded as foolish trifling with unimportant matters.

It is a most peculiar thing that those who take this view do not appear to have noticed that when, in Matthew 25, Jesus spoke of the coming of the Son of Man in his glory, the criterion of judgement whereby the sheep were to be separated from the goats was not narrowly personal at all. The important questions are about our record in the realm of social action—in relation to the hungry, the thirsty, the homeless, the poor, the sick and the imprisoned. It makes you think. At least you would *think* it would make you think. But closed minds don't think; they merely churn out clichés!

The fact is that we often use the words personal and social without any real understanding of their significance and relationship. We do not fully realize that our characteristic individualism is a quality which the Bible sees as the result of sin. True personality is the result of relationship. Consequently, in the purpose of God, the community is of supreme importance. This emphasis appears repeatedly in the Old Testament. God works through His people Israel. In the New Testament Jesus is the Founder of the New Israel which is the Church, and there is no salvation outside that Church.

A moment's reflection convinces us of the truth of this doctrine. Our experience bears it out. Our knowledge of God, our salvation, the very language of our devotion, all come from the community which He has created to be the channel of His communication. The old question about the hen and the egg is meaningless because you can't have one without the other. So personal faith and social relationship are indivisible and inter-dependent.

So closely is the quality of our social relationship linked with the health of our souls that Jesus plainly said that if on our way to worship we remembered we had fallen out with our brother, then it was no good entering the church. The first thing was to go and put things right: only then would worship be real and acceptable.

It would be a very great mistake to try to limit the range and application of this truth. A sense of social obligation and personal faith flourish together or both must atrophy. The implications of this for our evangelism are far-reaching. The extent to which they are being realized is to be seen in the emerging of a wider concept of ministerial training. It is no longer assumed that a minister is equipped for his task if he has received tuition in Bible study, theology, and Church history. Social studies are receiving more attention. The importance of pastoral counselling is being stressed. Training courses in industrial evanglism are being offered. Behind all this is the recognition that social involvement is a prerequisite of effective Christian mission. If we are to speak to men's needs, we must understand them. Such understanding will not alter the gospel we have to offer, but it will materially affect the manner in which we present it. Inevitably, as the range of study extends to embrace new and complicated disciplines, we find ourselves confronted with the need to call on the services of the expert.

A similar tendency is seen in the decision of some Churches whose membership is declining to undertake sociological surveys, designed to discover the reasons why people go to church, and why they stay away.

One possible reaction to all this is to turn away with the cry, 'Give me the simple gospel; my concern is with salvation, not with sociology'. Such a reaction, if it is followed up fervently, may lead to results. It may produce a harvest of happy individuals, selfishly shouting about their salvation, and resolved to have as little as possible to do with a sinful world, except to condemn it. But they are the sort of people whom the gospel numbers with the goats, not with the sheep.

This final fact, then, we must also underline: we must not make a false dichotomy between the personal and the social.

THEOLOGY AND PRACTICE

An impatient reader, if indeed he has persevered to this point, may well be muttering, 'It's all very well, all this theology, but when are we going to consider how it all works out in practice ?' The impatience is understandable. But there is good reason for starting with the theology. Without it we are likely very soon to be in trouble, as preachers often have been in the past. If one disastrous mistake is a theology unrelated to life, another equally dreadful error is the kind of preaching which is mere moral exhortation, or dabbling in social problems, unconnected with the strong redemptive message of the gospel. Unless our Christian citizenship is rooted in the theology of the New Testament it isn't Christian, and we have no right to talk about it in the pulpit.

Having laid the theological foundation of our case for a preaching which is relevant—that is, both biblical and topical—we may now profitably examine two common difficulties.

THE PROBLEM OF POLITICS

There can be no doubt that some preachers still fear that they may be charged with bringing politics into the pulpit. It is to be hoped that the general answer to this is now clear from what has been said earlier in the present article. But one or two further comments may be added.

Obviously the pulpit is not the place for party politics. Yet it is an oversimplification to say that no reference should ever be made to party political issues. There may be occasions when a great public issue has quite wrongly been made a party issue in parliament. If, as in the matter of capital punishment, an overwhelming consensus of Christian judgement has emerged as to the rights and wrongs of the issue, then there is no reason why the preacher should remain silent, and every reason why he should speak.

Frequently, of course, we are confronted by great issues upon which the parties are divided. Equally there is no common mind among Christians. To avoid all reference to such matters is to risk giving the impression that the Church does not care, or that preaching is irrelevant. What the preacher must do is to try to present a fair picture of those aspects of the matter on which Christians agree, and to indicate where there is sincere divergence of judgement. If he feels led to share with his hearers any personal conclusions which he believes God has laid upon his conscience to share, then no one is entitled to deny him this right. Providing always, of course, that the preacher eschews any desire to provoke contention and strife.

THE PROBLEM OF IGNORANCE

Many preachers feel deeply their limitations. Rather than venture upon any reference to big public issues without being fully informed, they prefer to remain silent. From one point of view this attitude is altogether commendable. Great disservice is done to the Church by preachers who air their views on social questions in ignorance of the real issues involved. Their efforts add nothing to our knowledge of God, and are an insult to those in their congregation who have taken the trouble to become better informed.

The equipment that the preacher needs in this regard is of two kinds, one general, the other more specific. The general preparation consists of a real and consistent attempt to keep abreast of the times. The preacher should read at least one reputable daily paper. He should not despise the contribution that television can make to his knowledge of current affairs. He should take a lively interest in the world about him just because it is God's world. It goes without saying that a certain discipline is involved in a sustained effort to keep abreast of the times. Such an effort is likely to flag and fail, unless it is rooted in a theological understanding of all that is involved in the call to preach the gospel.

The more specific aspect of the preacher's preparation in this regard must be the study of those important statements which emanate from the responsible courts and committees of the Churches. Methodists, for example, will be acquainted with the several Declarations of the Methodist Conference on Social Questions, as well as with the pronouncements on important issues made from time to time. The judgements of the British and World Councils of Churches too are readily available, and provide evidence of the thinking being done in the wider councils of Christendom.

It is not suggested that these judgements should always be slavishly accepted. Sometimes they will prove the starting point for further thinking. But we ought not to neglect the tools which are offered to us by the Church for the more effective discharge of our duty. Nor should we forget that one of the ways in which the Holy Spirit speaks to us is through the deliberations of those expert committees called into being to examine the social issues of our time in the light of the Christian gospel.

The pulpit ministry in many places would be much enhanced if groups of preachers would study some of the great contemporary issues together. In addition, preachers should seize any opportunities that exist for group discussion and debate. Not only is such fellowship immensely valuable in itself, but it serves to strengthen and support the ministry of the Word from the pulpit. The congregation plays no small part in the preparation of the sermon.

A PRACTICAL CONCLUSION

By way of conclusion let us imagine a team of preachers able to meet in fellowship at regular intervals. Let us suppose that they are able to plan out their preaching a year in advance. There is much that they will be able to do for each other. The calendar will be consulted. Any special observances, such as Hospital Sunday or Education Sunday, will be noted, as well as the great Christian Festivals. If there is some important campaign, such as Freedom from Hunger, the use of Harvest Festival Sunday in relation to the campaign can be discussed. Members of the group can make themselves responsible for approaching the various agencies which provide literature on the relevant subjects. Knowledge of appropriate books and literature can be pooled, not forgetting the value of books of prayers, and the careful choice of hymns which fit into the pattern of the service. A list may be drawn up of subjects which ought to receive attention. It may be useful to make certain broad headings, under which subjects may be grouped. These may include: work and leisure, home and family, moral welfare, drink and gambling, race relations, peace and international affairs.

Always the aim will be to make the preaching of the gospel relevant, to start with men where they are, and by God's grace to take them on to where He desires them to be. Out of such a ministry there are bound to come those important occasions of pastoral counselling which are real opportunities of evangelism. Of these none is more important than the chance to prepare young people for Christian marriage. This is a task which the Churches are taking more and more seriously. Much of the responsibility rests on the ordained ministry, but the job is so big that it must be shared with laymen and women who are informed and trained to help. To offer such help can be a powerful means of introducing young people to real religion, and demonstrating its relevance.

When Miss Molly Batten, the Principal of William Temple College, addressed the Assembly of the World Council of Churches in New Delhi in November 1961, she asked her hearers not to think of the Church as a place of retreat. Rather, she suggested, it was a depôt into which the soldiers of Christ come to get their rations and to hear their marching orders, before returning to the battle lines.

If, Mr Preacher, you think of them coming so, what word will you offer them, that they may go back into the world worthily equipped, to battle for their Lord?

3. Wanted—A World Outlook

By the REV. DOUGLAS W. THOMPSON

1. *THAT UNIQUE BOOK—THE BIBLE*

IN pre-communist China one of the Bible portions to sell best at temple-fairs was the single copy of Genesis. It sold on the Creation Story—which filled a gap in Chinese literature. Once, however, a Chinese customer brought his copy back and complained that he had been cheated. 'It is only the first two or three chapters,' he said, 'which talk about Creation; all the rest is about one family.'

In fact the book of Genesis is, as the Chinese said, the story of the Genesis of a family and a People, and it gives the story of the dramatic seven days in order to get a world—and some ancestors —for the children of Abraham. The beautiful early chapters really depend on chapter 11, verse 10, 'These are the generations of Shem.' In his turn Shem only matters because of Abraham and he only for the sake of Isaac and Jacob. They are important for the sake of the revelation in Genesis 32^{28}: 'Thy name shall be called no more Jacob but Israel.' Here, at last, the story has found its own internal significance, where the striving God finds the Chosen Man. The universal story of creation justifies itself when a people is possessed by and possessed of God. For the Bible creation's God is El-Elohe-Israel, God, the God of Israel.

Peoples, other than the Hebrews, have always complained that arrogance can hardly reach higher than this claim; but not only the Book of Genesis, the entire Bible is dyed throughout with this interpretation of existence. The argument is pursued, or assumed, all the way. The calling of a nation is held to require creation; the swarming peoples of the Babel story are foil to the one people. The meaning implicit in God's Word, 'Let us make man', is contained in the incident of one man wrestling with God at Jabok—day and night were made for this. The Bible saga runs: out of creation, man; out of man, tribes; out of tribes, the one tribe; out of the tribe, a man; within the man, a spiritual revolution; out of the revolution, a Chosen Race. The New Testament pattern is the same: from the Chosen Race, the Man; from the Man, the new international Chosen Race.

The story of nations all through the Bible, from the Philistines to the Romans, is recorded because they conditioned the life of Hebrew, Jew, and Christian. The rôle of the nations is symbolized by the presence of Pontius Pilate in the Creed; he survives in history by attachment to the Lord he killed. Sometimes the nations are condemned for persecuting The People. Sometimes God is depicted as manipulating the life of the nations to achieve a purpose in the life of His Own People. Sometimes The People are shown to be guardians of a treasure for all the nations. Whichever of these themes is dominant at any time, it is always true that it is not possible to know what God's purpose for his own People is without studying his treatment of the whole race.

This is the Bible 'point of view', and it is not possible to be a faithful preacher of the word of God without reckoning with the rise and fall of nations under God's over-arching command. When we preach, is it customary among us to relate our preaching to the drama of modern international life? Do we in fact adopt this 'scandalous' but biblical attitude to the world-story as our newspapers record it? The question is important for it is an integral part of our religious inheritance that we should. We are not Bible Preachers until we do.

We are meant to take such phrases as 'All things are yours' and in them see, not only that the riches of Christ are available for our own inner life, but that the stream of events is 'ours'. The birth of new nations, Burma, Ceylon, Ghana, Nigeria, Jamaica, relates to the fate of the People of God. The Old Testament prophets would not have missed one 'liberation' of this modern world, but would have claimed each for God and interpreted each in terms of His purpose for His own. Our world would have fitted them completely—the present-day dispersion of God's People is wider than they could have dreamed and the pace of world affairs so fast that the New Israel's life is for ever in turmoil.

In 1961 the Union of Burma established the Buddhist religion by law as the national faith, but minority pressures resulted in Christianity being listed as a tolerated faith. Today the Christian Church finds itself freer in Burma than ever before—because of the establishment of Buddhism! In the same year the Republic of Italy—for the first time in Italian history—gave recognition to the Methodist Church as a voluntary corporation within the law. A Bill also passed through the Houses of Parliament according State Pension rights to our Ministers. In 1962, on the birth of Jamaica as an independent State, one of our Ministers composed the nation's first National Anthem. What would Amos, Jeremiah, and Micah have made of these three events—tiny fragments of our world picture?

These sample situations differ; they are three situations in a biblical sense. A non-Christian State took an action which directly affected the life of the Church, though the State did not intend to protect Christianity but Buddhism. The Italian government took political action to demonstrate its independence of hierarchical pressure groups, and picked up the life of Protestantism, as it were by accident, into its decision. The Rev. Hugh Sherlock took action, as a Christian poet and a patriot, which will affect the life of a nation for generations. Here are three of the Bible ways of Church-nation contact, alive in our world.

We are accustomed to the type of action seen in Jamaica, in which the Church does something for the people; but it is quite unbiblical to see the hand of God only in that type of interaction. The Bible view is that the Burmese and Italian governments were also subject to His will. God's People are never isolated from God's world—He plans all.

We play with this idea in daily life. Our children arrive at Sunday School eating chocolate which owes its raw material to Ghana or Nigeria. If our children did not eat chocolate a nation's economy would split. Our Youth Clubs change from 'Rock and Roll' to the 'Twist' and as they do so they give a noisy expression to the fact that the United States of America dominates the life of the Western World. These instances are pregnant with theological significance. What is God's plan for a world of primary producers and industrial users, or a world in which cultural patterns flow down from one power source, when the Bible has shown us that His total strategy is one and for His People?

Most preachers at some time tell their congregations that the on-going life of the Church is the sequel to the Acts of the Apostles—and the claim is true and verifiable—but too few tell their hearers that the inclusive kaleidoscope of world affairs is the sequel to the whole Bible story. We would have less trouble from small religious sects and sub-Christian groups if we did this more often. It is not for us to find Mr Kruschev in the Book of the Revelation—which would be to make a parody of the Bible doctrine of history—but it *is* ours to delve into world affairs, and to reveal the mighty acts of God as He works out His one purpose. We cannot play tricks with the Book of Daniel, but there are moments of equation in history. 'In the year that King Uzziah died I saw the Lord' matches 'In the first year of the Chinese Democratic People's Republic I saw the Lord.'

The Christian preacher is necessarily a world-scrutineer; the Bible, indeed, has some terrible things to say about those who neglect this duty. It is not our business to protect our people from the blast of world affairs or to divert them from the painful sight of world change. A preacher could not read, for example, the sixth chapter of Jeremiah and then offer his congregation a neat essay on a tidy little theme, to distract them from the threat of 'the bomb'. It is that great world outside, hungry, riddled with disease, print-blind and, so often, dragooned by exploiters which is in travail with God's purpose for the Church and the race.

Preachers can often claim that they 'preach Christ' and mean by it that they despise those who introduce the world's affairs into the pulpit. St Luke also preached Christ, but he prefaced his tremendous evangelical pamphlet with true historic thunder. 'Now in the 15th year of the reign of Tiberius Caesar, Pontius Pilate being Governor of Judea, and Herod being Tetrarch of Galilee and his brother Tetrarch of the region of Itruraea and Trachonicus and Lysanias Tetrarch of Abiline, in the High Priesthood of Annas and Caiaphas, the word of God came to John, son of Zacharia in the wilderness.'

So history is part of eternity and eternity only known to men in moments of history—as is majestically set out in St John's Gospel, chapter 13. 'Now before the Feast of the Passover, Jesus knowing that his hour was come that he should depart out of this world unto the Father, having loved his own which were in the world, he loved them to the end. And during supper, the devil having already put into the heart of Judas Iscariot, Simon's son, to betray him, Jesus, knowing that the Father had given all things into his hands, and that he came from God and goeth unto God, riseth from supper, and layeth aside his garments; and he took a towel and girded himself.'

This is purest Bible-method, used by St John. The world's destiny is concentrated on a towel, while a baleful world outside is preparing a trial and a cross. Point and counterpoint, dark and light, matched together reveal the truth. God's purpose lies over the whole; the tug of evil is at the very heart of the embryo Church, Caiaphas is sleepless through hate, ignorant soldiers are being detailed for a disgusting duty. These are all in the wings of the eternal stage, set in time. At the centre of the stage is the Master, knowing all these things, kneeling at Peter's dusty feet.

It is easy for our minds to skid over such a phrase as 'Before the foundation of the world' but to the Bible it is precise, earnest truth, the clue to all history, 'I made a world to get you.' Do we preach after this fashion?

2. *WATCHMEN TO THE HOUSEHOLD OF GOD*

The sweep of historical processes being the continuation of the Bible story, the life of the Church being the continuation of the Acts of the Apostles, our Lord Himself and the first evangelists having worked conscious of the wider activities of God, the preacher is necessarily Watchman to the Household of God in his own generation. He must, as Jesus said, discern the signs of the times. He has to be a student of the world's affairs for deeper reasons than those whose profession it is to comment on them for the newspapers or radio. To the professional commentator what is happening in the world is simply the raw material of his work; for the preacher events are a matter of the revelation of God's activity, and he sees them as interwoven into the pattern of God's intention for His People.

To be a Watchman to the Household of God is to continue the vocation of the Prophets; and preachers know that so much of the Bible's prophecy is analysis of contemporary events which, in the form of the 'burdens', declared to the Holy Nation the activities of surrounding nations in relation to Israel's life—it was news commentary. 'For thus hath the Lord said unto me, "Go, set a watchman; let him declare what he seeth; and when he seeth a troop, horsemen in pairs, a troop of asses, a troop of camels, he shall hearken diligently with much heed".' To give heed and diligent attention to the world is an essential of the preacher's life.

How much have preachers noted, in this last decade? More than 600,000,000 people have gone out from under the Union Jack since the end of World War II, and set up their own banners. 'To your tents, O Israel!' The United Nations has passed from being a power structure dominated by the victors of World War II to become a forum of many nations with an anti-Western bias —and here lies the key to the bad Press it has had in the West in recent times. The little State of Mali, with a tiny population, now has a vote in world affairs as powerful as that of the dominant United States of America. Let him who reads the prophet Nahum consider this. In the last decade at least four new States have been born with constitutions based upon Islam and two have been founded on Buddhism, but in this time of nation-building not one State has emerged based upon Christianity.

In this period many of the new States have owed much of their beginnings to the leadership of Christian men, but in a number of them the coming of independence has been followed immediately by a purge of Christian leadership, and the rise to power of more extreme thinkers. This is largely due to the fact that this new world sees Christianity as the Western regional religion, and therefore a thing to be repudiated with other Western things. Indeed, it is true that the numerical strength of Christianity does lie in the European-American world, while the new nations are growing up outside that world, in the six-sevenths of the world which is coloured. If Christianity is presented to the world's peoples as 'white', domesticated into European life, its future must be to be 'left as a booth in a vineyard, as a lodge in a garden of cucumbers, as a besieged city' (Isa. 1^8). There is real danger of that happening unless the 'white' Christian is told these things.

The preacher who cannot see 'a troop of horses' in Central Europe, 'a troop of camels' in the United Arab Republic, is not looking; and if he is not looking he cannot assess and speak of the will of God in the modern world. If a preacher who does not watch the world attempts to speak of the will of God he will be in danger, either of talking of little things or of merely echoing the judgements of better men than himself, who, in their day, did watch the tide of affairs and judge it, but whose judgements are now out of date. One of the commonest examples of this error is for the modern preacher to speak of the world mission of Christianity in terms of the late Nineteenth Century. Then it was thought of as a march out, like a new crusade, from a strong Western base into an inarticulate and darkling world. Our hymn-book is rich in such ideas. As Livingstone tramped Central Africa the interpretation was valid but today the Faith has no longer a base; it is a thin scattering of hard-won strong points everywhere on the world map. Not like a mighty army but like guerrilla forces moves the Church of God, and the preacher who gives the old interpretation is cheating.

The matter involves deeply the integrity of the preacher's message. Even if a preacher maintains that his business is to appeal with an individualized call to individual men with an offer of individual salvation—and who would deny it ?—he cannot do this without being aware that both the Bible and daily life declare God's purposes to be wider than the one person. Man, to whom the preacher speaks, is set tightly into a world, and he cannot be extracted from it; his thought forms belong to it, he will vote in the next election, his wages will be involved in the next fall in tin prices.

The preacher will therefore find that he cannot make his simple appeal unless he knows the world which encases the man. He may choose such a text as 'Look and live', and endeavour to turn the man's mind to the Cross; but the man knows that millions of men in more than half the world look to the Hammer and Sickle in order to live. In the other half, countless men and women are quite sure they must look only to economic opportunity. In the same world Ghanaian boys and girls are singing 'Nkrumah never dies', or 'Nkrumah does no wrong' to the tune of 'Old soldiers never die', while our preacher is saying 'Jesus saves'. If the overtones of that world are ignored by the evangelist we cannot be surprised if the hearers think the preaching irrelevant.

God is working in this same world in which the Hammer and Sickle have become a rallying symbol and the wealth of technological revolution is transforming living standards. This is Bible teaching. 'The cattle on a thousand hills' in this world today is the oil in a thousand wells, the steel in a thousand mills. The preacher is concerned in economics, big-business, national revolutions, new racial alignments. The condition of the world at any one moment is a theological factor in that moment. The preacher cannot preach without mastering it.

Much of the pain of being one of God's preachers is that we must scan the world from the watchtower of faith. There are bound to be times when the Bible preacher looks around him in sheer anguish and cries in the face of God, 'What are You doing?' He will see, for instance, that Eastern European boys cannot get into the universities because they are Christian; he will see that the old anti-semitism can rise again in a 'Christian' land to torment God's ancient people. If he shakes his fist in God's face demanding the 'why' of these things he is no more blaspheming than were some of the prophets who went before him. The preacher who pretends all this does not matter is the faithless one. Better be Jonah, petulant under his castor oil tree, angrily saying, 'It is better for me to die than to live', than to pretend that God's mercies in Nineveh have nothing to do with us. If a preacher watches the news, weighs the event, slaves to see the pattern of God's purpose, he will not miss God's caustic comfort. 'Doest thou well to be angry?' It was God who prepared the worm.

3. THE PREACHER AS INTERPRETER OF WORLD NEWS

The preacher, while searching for the meaning in world events, in our modern world has to cope with the fact that his congregations are deluged with news. They are exposed to the full gale of partisan information from the moment when they read the morning paper to the time of the Late Night News Summary. The external facts of the acts of God the Holy Spirit are deployed before them with interpretations every day, but they are not deployed by those who present them as acts of God; and congregations, all too often, lack the theological basis of knowledge which alone can draw out from the movements of history their real significance.

It is as though a great wall map had been chopped up into fragments as small as confetti, and snowed upon them from above. They see the rain of confetti, but no one has told them that the tiny fragments make a map. The preacher's main interest lies in the fact that he knows the bits are parts of a whole; a knowledge he has acquired from the Bible. He starts from the proposition that 'God is not the God of the dead but of the living'. Consequently he bears the heavy responsibility of being Mr Interpreter as well as being Watchman; and very often he has to interpret—and correct—those other interpreters who have an interest in exploiting the news.

The sin of propagandizing is one of the great sins of such a civilization as ours, and it is found everywhere. One has only to reflect that such a fine word as 'indoctrination' has in our times become a dirty word, and that the word 'propaganda' itself once was a noble word (it is still the official name of the central office in the Roman Catholic Church for missionary effort) to see the downward drift of standards which occurs when news is plentiful and godly interpretation scarce.

During the Sino-Japanese war of the 1930's one of our missionaries who listened regularly to the Tokyo news broadcasts repeatedly heard that the town in China in which he was living had been captured by the Japanese Imperial Army. On one occasion he heard the radio give the text of the speech of welcome given by the mayor of the town to the incoming 'liberators'. He was, at that time, mayor of the town himself and very busy trying to persuade its citizens to spare the lives of Japanese prisoners of war! This is a gross example of news as a weapon of war, and there are those who think that it is only used that way by 'lesser breeds'.

A preacher would be well advised to check this comfortable delusion for himself by listening some evening to the news in English from London, Moscow, Paris, Prague, and the U.S. Forces' Voice of America. He will see at once that news is war even now in times of peace, and he will long for some source of unadulterated information. This is particularly true of news about the conflict over colour, and about the life and health of the new nations of the world. It is a good sign today that more and more preachers telephone or write to the Mission House for accurate information on such news.

The classical Methodist resistance to using the pulpit for politics has this advantage, that it prevents the pulpit from being used as a party platform; but it also has its disadvantages, which are highlighted by the way in which a German Bishop, or the leader of a Methodist Church in Africa, will cause an encyclical letter—on some current issue which affects the life of the nation and Church—to be read in the pulpits. This is a veritable pastoral use of the pulpit, and part of the life of the Church since the beginning. It is this use which preachers might help to see revived.

The popularity of such programmes in television as 'Panorama' and 'This Week', matched with the popularity of travel and anthropological programmes on both sound and vision, constitutes a sign and a portent for preachers. The people want the background to world news—something in them tells them they need it, and that something is the work of the Holy Spirit. There never was a time when people were more whole-world minded than this. (Even here, however, a comparison between an American and a European programme on the Common Market would show how much an explanation of an event can vary with the sources of origin.)

Nevertheless, a new profession has grown up in our times, and national personalities have emerged who make it the serious concern of their lives to give the nation sincere and accurate estimates of what is happening round us. Some would say they have stolen the preacher's thunder, but this is not so; they are the preacher's allies and he must press onward beyond where they stop.

The preacher has a standard of judgement which they do not possess. It is too much to expect that they should believe with a whole heart that God is at work in the divisions of modern Europe or the rise of nations in Africa. They do not begin with the belief that every motion of the world's life is under sovereign direction. It is not for them to read the dissolution of empire as judgement or the rise of new power blocs as a reflection of the immutable laws of God. It is not for them to say, for example, that the institution of slavery in Jamaica bore within its womb from the beginning the birth of a nation. This is the preacher's business: so he comments on the comments on the news, exposing Divine action.

News commentators also search for motives behind events. They may see the drive of self-interest in the 'cold war' or in the pressure of international salesmanship, but the preacher knows that these things—though they are real—are, as it were, the stage properties of the drama, and that the real drive is hidden in the mind of God. And God is always at work, 'making the wrath of men to praise him', and pushing mankind on—to its original destiny as the Holy Family. The preacher begins by knowing— not just thinking—that 'the earth shall be filled with the glory of God as the waters cover the sea'. Because of this he knows also that there can be no human movement which in the long or short run does not pay tribute to the All High God. It shall, willingly or not, conform to His plan and, as it develops—and long before it reaches its final confluence with the plan in God's mind— evolve some features which reflect the truth, beauty, and goodness of God. It is, for example, this fact which lies behind the astonishment with which some observers return from Russia or China, and tell us of things they found there lovelier than those they see at home.

The preacher, therefore, cannot imitate certain news commentators in sweeping whole movements under the carpet, in the pretence that they do not exist. Again, he cannot pronounce great human drives as being totally bad. (If there is a 'totally bad' area in human experience, where is God in relation to that experience?) It is the preacher's duty to comb through each movement, looking for its values and estimating its total impact on God's final plan. Such objective scrutiny is a biblical discipline.

Doing this he might conclude, for instance, that nationalism has done more to prevent the obliteration of little peoples suffering the impact of modern civilization than any other force. He might conclude that Communism has done more to stir the social conscience of the world since 1917 than any other ideology. He will certainly discover that the Islamic attitude to colour-bar is healthier than that of popular Christianity today. He will probably conclude too that the sweep of materialism, so much condemned, has in fact transformed life for millions of hungry people, and saved the lives of thousands of infants who without it would have died within a year of birth.

The text, 'The foolishness of God is wiser than men', assumes a new relevance when the preacher studies his world this way and interprets it to his folk. To know, for example, that the whole of the Buddhist world and the whole of the Communist world (one man in the world of every three is Buddhist and one in four is Communist, at least in allegiance) is committed to the proposition that God does not exist, and yet to know that so much of our scientific progress today is based on Russia or Japan is to pass out of fear into triumph. 'The weakness of God is stronger than men.' Men may bow God out of the front door, but He returns by the window.

When the preacher interprets the world in this fashion our young folk will cease to grumble at long sermons and the relevance of the pulpit will return. The young want their world explained by their spiritual leaders. It is a tragedy, to take only one issue, that our Lord said, 'of that time knoweth no man', and yet Christian young people are so often afraid that some drunken American airman or trigger-happy Muscovite can, by wrongly pressing a button, end the world. God will end God's world and He will do so when He has finished His perfect work in it. Here biblical theology is news, desperately needed news.

There could be a day when people, inside and outside the Church, look forward as eagerly to the sermon as they now wait for 'Panorama' or 'This Week', and for the right reason—that God's preachers have begun to preach.

4. THE ASPIRATIONS OF ALL MEN

The Bible has a great deal to say of the religious life of those peoples whose life made a framework for the development of the Chosen People. Quite a picture of contemporary beliefs can be built up from the writings of the prophets. 'Bel boweth down, Nebo stoopeth; their idols are upon the beasts and upon the cattle.' This picture of the tottering might of the great gods of mighty Babylon is both religious and political commentary in one; but the point of the commentary, in both realms, is in the following verses: 'Even to old age I am He, and even to hoar hairs will I carry you; I have made and I will bear; yea, I will carry and

I will deliver.' This is true preacher's commentary, with religious life and statecraft inextricably entwined. The prophets realized vividly that a nation's life and its religion are one. It is a realization which is one of the key factors in our own times. Here is one more place in which the Bible is as modern as we are.

There is a real danger today of Christian preachers who do not watch the world going on thinking the thoughts of their fathers and preaching as though Christianity had the world to itself. Thirty years ago a great deal was written about the decay of the other great world religions—echoes of this, too, are still to be found in our own hymn-book—and it was commonly felt that nothing but Christianity could stand up to the erosion of the new age of science. It was expected that cultural unity, technical development, and our religion made together a force with which no other thought system but ours could cope. It was a great illusion.

As Latourette has pointed out in his history, the year 1914 saw the Christian religion world-dominant for the first time but it was a short-lived dominance, a fleeting moment. World War II, the decline of imperial Western power and the birth of nationalism, combined with the tonic effects of the success of Christian evangelism itself and the Christian discovery of the sacred writings of the old faiths, brought revival to Buddhism, Hinduism, and Islam. They became again world forces.

Other forces with power to sway people's minds arose also. Some would classify Communism as a new faith; and in the East there has been a proliferation of new religions, hundreds in Japan alone. In Africa, where no great ethnic faith has its roots, where people have been given up to the diffused light of Animism and ancestor worship (belief in the life and potency of all things, which crystallizes in totems, charms, and witchcrafts) even these lowlier forms of religion, which would have been expected to die first, and from which in fact Christianity has made most of its gains, have revived. Some leaders of new Africa—many of them possessing modern education—have gone back to libations, sorcery, and incantation. There are examples of the spirits being consulted before a new engineering project sponsored by United Nations technical aid has been begun. The copper mines of Rhodesia and oil drillings of Nigeria can be associated with a strangled chicken offered in sacrifice.

Buddhism is followed by a third of the world's people and Islam has proved itself a powerful nation-building force, so that those European minds which have thought that modern Christianity has only the one competitor, materialism, are in fact wrong. Materialism has stimulated old competitors to new vigour. One has only to notice how gingerly the Communist powers deal with the Islamic States and how even Chinese Communism stalked Tibet under a religious banner, to see that Christianity is not alone as a religious power in the world. Some of the nations in which the old faiths are dominant, largely non-aligned states, are among the world's most noisy protagonists. Christianity is weak in its own traditional centres and has minority status in the new succession states of the old empires. Three of the great religions have more part in the rebuilding of their own nations than Christianity has with us.

If the old faiths have shown enough resilience to come back in this sort of world, if they can offer protection to their peoples from the winds of secularism (and this is their claim), the situation is one in which the preacher must seriously look for divine meaning.

Has God spoken through Mohammed and Gautama? If in real fact the devout Pakistani, Egyptian, and Burmese pray regularly and mount great national religious occasions which assert spiritual values in national life, is it time to say again, 'I have not found so great faith, no, not in Israel'? Does the divine plan have a place for these other faiths? The question is not one to be dismissed by a superior wave of the hand.

The preacher must cope with the fact that day by day millions of people live by faith in the other religions. Children are born, people pass through times of sickness, loved ones die and people are stayed by their own faith. The land dries up and crops wither, or floods sweep the countryside and swallow whole villages, and the folk find comfort.

It is the preacher's business to communicate a faith to live by, and where vast numbers of people are finding every day in some other religious system courage to live, a refuge in storm and laughter in tragedy, there is something the Christian preacher cannot ignore.

This is not to say that the Christian Way is not the crown of all religions; it is not to say that the Buddhist is to be left without Christ; it is not to say that the Moslem possesses all that God, the All Merciful, has prepared for him. Still less is it to say that the revivals of animistic voodoo and witchcraft are anything but frightened souls running for any port in a storm. It *is* to say, however, that God has not left himself without witness in any place. It is to say that the Buddha's Eightfold Path has produced some very lovely people. It is to say that the European Christian who feels himself stranded among a mass of unbelievers has millions of fellow-believers on the path of prayer in India and the East. It is to say that the proper study for the man of faith is faith—wherever it is found.

One has only to see a decent, middle-class Burmese kneeling in a temple saying the classical formula of prayer, 'I take refuge in the Buddha; I take refuge in the Law; I take refuge in the Order', to feel the cords of sympathy which bind him to the Christian—to the Christian who, in his time of need, borrows from the Jew and cries, 'I will lift up mine eyes to the hills; from whence cometh my help? My help cometh from the Lord, which made heaven and earth.' The Christian is on sure ground claiming the Creator as his help, while the Buddhist cry, at the last, is a cry to himself to aid himself (for Buddha said there was none other aid); yet the bond of sympathy between the two men is a gift of God. The preacher must know these faiths and the hearts of the men and women who cherish them. He should know the outlines of these faiths but, even more important, he should know the actual system of daily living which each faith gives to the people who practise it (often a very different picture). In doing so he will quickly find that many British people he knows are unwittingly living by the tenets of one of the other religions.

5. CLINICAL REPORTS FOR THE PREACHER

The Christian preacher proclaims a Gospel of salvation on the authority of Jesus, who claimed to be the Saviour of the world. It is therefore of the highest importance to him to have actual case-studies of people being saved. The testimony meeting, which is now out of fashion in Methodism, had great usefulness in this matter. St John said, 'That which our eyes have seen and our hands handled'; he also claimed, 'We know we have passed from death into life because we love the brethren.' The Living Word can only be confirmed in the living situation. It is unfair to proclaim what cannot be demonstrated. Much of the weakness of modern preaching lies just here. Shy of 'results' we tend to make statements which can only be proven by results, and it is not remarkable that people cease to listen.

A preacher himself needs to be strengthened by 'signs confirming', 'fruits of grace' appearing and 'souls for his hire', and it may well be that the decline in the number of preachers and the drift out of the ministry are partly to be explained by the sterility of preaching. Encouragement is in short supply. Often this is due to preachers looking for their results on too narrow a field. Jesus told his men, when their hearts were filled with doubt, to see him talking to a foreign woman by a non-Jewish well: 'Lift up your eyes and look on the fields that are white already unto harvest.' When they lifted their eyes they looked into a Samaritan village— which contained at least five adulterous men—and to which they would never have dreamed of looking for the harvest they expected to ripen in Jewry. But the story ends in two testimonies: 'He told me all that I ever did', and 'For we have heard for ourselves and know that this is indeed the Saviour of the world.' Not even the disciples could argue with that. There is no future for the preacher with the muck rake, whose eyes are only on the churches in which he labours and who thinks only of the Church overseas as something which once a year makes a financial demand on the congregations. It is very different for the preacher who realizes that the overseas work is the 'test-bed' of the universal claims of Christ.

In recent years the Conference of our Church has heard records of a small decline in membership; it is not so well known that in every one of those years the overseas Districts have shown an increase. Methodism is not declining, it is simply finding the going hard in Britain; an average of ten thousand new full members overseas each of those years has always given our whole Church the edge of advance. Moreover, the record of members in training has always filled up, as the new members have moved from one column in the return to the final column. These new people have been won out of the background of world revolution and powerfully competing faiths of which we have already spoken. Indeed, the places which stand out as fields of conquest are remarkable. The seething-pot of Central Africa has been one for some years, the stamping ground of Mau Mau has produced a harvest, people from primitive cultures have been matched by sons of some of the world's greatest cultures. The Chinese business man has found the same grace as the forest dweller of Borneo and the simple folk of the Zambesi Valley. This surely is the meaning in our hymn, 'When new triumphs of Thy Name swell the raptured hosts above, may I feel a kindred flame.'

In one of our Districts one person in every twenty is a class leader, and the ratio of local preachers is higher than that. In all the Districts together more than a million boys and girls are in our schools, the number of babies born in our hospitals in one year would more than fill the Albert Hall with the noisiest audience it ever contained. The majority of the overseas candidates for the ministry are in training together with Anglican, Presbyterian students and students of other Communions. Lay training is a regular part of District life in most of the Districts, and youth work is a District priority. In some places we are training young men in skills with which to earn a living and witness to Christ in their daily work, such as the farm project in Southern Rhodesia and the co-operative work in Haiti. Elsewhere our Church is in the forefront of social and scientific research; as at Ilesha, for children, and at Uzuakoli, for those suffering from leprosy.

Nor has our Church the monopoly of these gains; our story is also the story of the other branches of the Church and with those other branches we work in harmony. In Italy our ministers exchange stations with the ministers of the Calvinist Waldensian Church. Partnership is the rule of life in a way in which it is unknown in Great Britain, and this 'new Christendom' is becoming very impatient with the West, which itself will not move to union and which puts brakes on its daughter Churches as they do so.

Mention any feature in the Ministry of Jesus as recorded in St Mark and it can be paralleled in the life of the overseas Church. To heal the sick, to drive out demons (in the most literal sense), to feed the hungry, to preach to the poor; it is all there and yet, all too often, these mighty works of grace are fobbed off on to one Sunday in the year—and that, one on which many local preachers do not preach—and this in the land from which the message went overseas. It is this material which the preacher needs week by week, right round the Church Year. At this point we err, not because we do not know the Scriptures, but because we will not recognize the finger of God touching our contemporary world.

There is more to it than this. Every time the preacher enters his pulpit he does so under the command of a Lord who claimed the world. We are the servants of a Master who is universal or nothing. Our most pointed and narrowly aimed appeal to men and women to believe rests solidly on Jesus' universal claim. There is no British Saviour whose efficacy is specially for Anglo-Saxons; the Briton finds mercy from every man's Christ, and from Him alone.

It follows that if Christ cannot save the African, the Indian, the Chinese, then the Briton cannot be saved; for Christ's claim to save any man is dependent on His claim to be Saviour of all. A

British Christian, therefore, can kneel to pray through the Name of Christ only if he is confident that in fact Christ is saving men of all lands and under all conditions. Every prayer he makes is underwritten by people of other races and places. They 'set to their seal that Jesus is true'.

The World Church is the demonstration that the Faith is not an evocation of the spirit of the Western lands—a sort of local myth—but is a genuine intervention of God in the life of mankind. The Saviour of the young men in Oxford University's John Wesley Society is also the Saviour of the Lushai tribesman in Upper Burma. He has found his men and women in the rondavels of African villages. If Christ could not enter and win men in the Chindwin Valley of Burma and in huts on the shores of Lake Kariba, then the brightest English youth could have no reliance on Him. Indeed any such young man has the right to challenge Christ to demonstrate His universality under all conditions before venturing his life upon the Way of Jesus. To take a recent case. A Communist journalist in Russia has recently complained, because of the number of Christians in the universities, that 'a good education is no guarantee in modern Russia that a man is a true atheist'. The Western graduate Christian can be grateful for this bit of pregnant apologetic. After forty-five years of militant anti-godism it is good to know that some Russian intelligentsia find in Jesus their Master.

The wide-awake Christian preacher is like a good doctor who wants to read in the *Lancet* the clinical reports of what new medicines and treatments actually achieve wherever they are used. The preacher wants to know what sort of graces, what sort of changes, Christ makes in men whose life-patterns are different from his own. For the preacher *The Kingdom Overseas*, to name only one source of report, is more than just a 'missionary magazine'; it is a fount of professional information. One veteran missionary with wide experience has said that for him one of the greatest evidences for the truth of the Faith is the amazing similarity in character-structure of the Methodist Ministry all round the world. He finds that these men must have been exposed to some moulding force which has worked commonly on them all.

6. *THE FOUR SEAS WITHIN FIVE HYMNS*

The preacher's world is an enormous one. He has to deal with a Bible which is a world book, he has to be watchman and interpreter to the People of God, his heart has to find sympathy with men and women of faith in whatever faith they have been reared, he has to study and make known the triumphs of God's grace 'in many a soul and mine'. This fivefold function of the preacher comes to its finest flower when he leads a people, willing to be led, by worship into the presence of God; and only world-worthy worship is good enough for even the most remote village or the most sedate town congregation. It is not the site on which we preach but the magnitude of the grace of God which should determine our pattern of worship.

Whether a congregation meets in a tiny 'Ebenezer' on a country by-way or in a grubby Victorian chapel in a street of terraced houses, the preacher's first task is to invoke, in that place, the actual presence of God. The God whom we invite to be present is He who knows the last secret cupboard in the Kremlin and the thoughts in the mind of a Stone Age Christian in Africa. This is what we are doing when we sing, 'Jesus, stand among us in Thy risen power': and its full significance would frighten us to death were we not staled by long custom, as newly won African Christians or persecuted Eastern European young Christians are not.

Unless we are completely deluded, God comes at our call; and that we are not deluded is testified by millions of fellow Christians, and by the 'devout men' in other religions. We can testify that men have called and still call upon the Living God and find Him, for God's nature is like that of Jesus Christ. For us it is God who says, 'Bring him to Me.' The nature of God is one and unchanging; for all men and for each He is the same, whether the man who calls is Christian or not. There is not one God for the Christian and another for the non-Christian, neither is there one mood of God's mind for the Christian and a less lovely one for the non-believer. The difference between the believer and the non-believer is that the Christian knows God as the God and Father of Our Lord Jesus Christ, while the non-Christian experiences the mercy of God through a veil of ignorance. He encounters a God he does not know, and attributes the encounter to a god who does not exist—or to a part of himself with which he thinks he only meets in meditation. 'Ye worship that which ye know not: we worship that which we know: for salvation is from the Jews.' The Christian community is the New Israel, and as Jesus pointed to the Jewish worship as validating the worship of Samaritans, so in our age it is Christian worship which validates the non-Christian.

The fact of Christian worship being offered continually in heaven and on earth is the foundation underneath the whole world's unending but fear-ridden prayers. It is as though faithful Christian people, who know God in Jesus Christ, counter-signed the petitions of myriads of people who only know an unseen Someone. In Romans 8[26] we are taught that our own inabilities in prayer are made good for us by the work of the Holy Spirit. In Christian prayer we, in our turn, assist in this work of the Holy Spirit. This is one of the ways in which the Church is the 'Spirit-filled Community'.

There is a strange power in corporate Christian prayer. Once upon a time there were only a few hundred men and women in the Near East who really knew the Person to whom all prayers ascend, but their conviction that their God desired that all men should be saved made them one with masses of people who prayed in ignorance. The solidarity of all human life made that little Christian community the world's path of access to truth. In them humanity, which prayed to a thousand gods, stood before the True God. The little aspirations of the world, the stumbling beliefs in Someone hearing prayers, reached heaven and the God of love, borne on the eagle wings of such men and women as could with intelligence pray, 'O Saviour of the world, let the pitifulness of Thy great mercy loose us from our sins, we humbly beseech Thee.' As the Hebrew priest entered the Holy Place for the whole people, so the Christian Community enters the Holy Place for a whole world. The doctrine of the Priesthood of All Believers is a fact of human solidarity, not a mere scholar's fancy.

The preacher's task in worship, therefore, begins by making sure that Mrs Smith, who is always there, and Mr Brown, who plays the organ, realize that they are at work in worship for the whole world. They must know that their prayers carry up to the Eternal Throne the sick and needy of that world. Will their hearts move out in sympathy—for instance—to meet the Indian mother who has a sick child, who has already sacrificed at a dozen altars for her child's sake and who now wonders, since the child is still ill, which of the gods she has offended?

One thing is absolutely certain, that the prayers in that chapel are matched by God, in time and concern, to the needs of men and women who know not how to pray for themselves—both in unevangelized lands and in minds which are unevangelized at home. God is at one and the same time out in the world alongside every man, and present where His people intercede for the world.

He knows that Indian mother by name, and can pour the little congregation's love straight into her lap, a balm from heaven.

In the ancient Chinese Empire there was but one altar of sacrifice to the God of Heaven—the Temple of Heaven in Peking —and on it only the Emperor could make sacrifice and prayer, which he did for the whole 'Hundred Names'—the entire people. So too the Christian community stands in the world as the Temple of Heaven, and the prayer and his congregation are the Royal Priesthood praying for the Hundred Names. Our labours in Christ are always twofold: we declare the unknown God to men in order that their manhood may be perfected in Him; we pray also, on behalf of all unknowing men and women, to the God whom we know whenever we worship. Such prayer in our chapels can be a converting instrument at the other side of the world, and it is always a Christian 'charity', in the fine, age-old sense, bestowed upon a needy world.

Worship is not just five hymns, two lessons, a short prayer and a long, with the sermon as major item; it is spiritual redemption, it is the service of the world-altar, it is pregnant with meaning for people we shall never see on earth. A Chinese proverb says, 'All within the four seas are brothers'; so too our worship is to enclose the four seas within the five hymns, and the tiniest congregation can be the heart of the world.

When we look at worship with this universal perspective we may well think that its preparation is a harder task than sermon preparation. It is certainly as important. But just as the study of the world's affairs is a major source of inspiration and guidance for our preaching, so also it is a major source of material for our worship.

During the last war a Jewish Chaplain to the Forces attended Evensong in an Anglican church. He afterwards told his Christian friends that there was very little in the whole service which he could not, as a Jew, share. For the beauty of that act of worship owed a tremendous debt to the old faith of Judaism. There are other debts which the preacher may well incur. He can, for instance, read the English translations of Chinese Taoist and Buddhist literature and he will find in them many heart-warming thoughts and phrases worthy of inclusion in worship. 'Great in Mercy, Great in Pity, Hearer of the world's prayers, hear my cry.' This is the standard prayer of women approaching Kuan Yin and, used in Christian worship, comes fresh to the Englishman's mind, while at the same time it links our worship into millions of lives overseas. Or, what could be nobler for use in prayer than the Confucian definition of the True God? 'O, Thou above Whom there is none; to Whose right and left none may stand, Thou alone worthy to be named as God, great art Thou.' That cry is three thousand years old, at least. From the same source we get a statement that God is good, in the words 'When man seeks to hurt man Heaven resists; were Heaven to wish to hurt man the very grass would not grow.' These are but fragments of a vast literature which awaits the adventurous preacher seeking new ways to bring life to jaded worship.

So the preacher conducting worship has a high duty and a high privilege which are his, by gift from God, through the wider world and the wider Church. While he cannot be true to his vocation without including the world in worship—and especially in prayer —he also is provided, because of God's abiding presence in every place and age, with a mine of rich material. By including both in worship he confers upon it status, dignity and purpose for the smallest congregations, and he rebukes the often too facile worship of self-centred churches.

He has the key to the worship literature of the whole world, in good translations—especially of the sacred books of the East— and by using them he can give them a new value which only Christian usage can provide. (See Note at end of this article, on p. 92.) Out of these riches he can bring the gifts of the nations into the Kingdom of Christ, and so refresh his people. This refreshment also includes that which can be had from the worship of the contemporary Church in other lands. The Church of South India prayers are already finding a place in European worship, and the contribution of West Indian music is not to be missed. A study of the Eastern Orthodox Church worship would be for many preachers a rediscovery of the significance of the work of the Holy Spirit.

7. *THE AMBASSADOR*

A man is no more than a scribe if he only knows 'about' religion. He is a Christian preacher when he knows God, and in conscious union with Him goes out into God's world to find others. Only so can he offer up his life to nurture others in their experience of God. Such a preacher is a servant to the whole world, wherever he is called to work; and he also holds the whole world in fee as he seeks insight into his vocation. In contrast the preacher who is 'not keen on missions', and whose mind does not reach out to embrace the whole Church and the whole world of stumbling mankind, just is not like the God he professes to proclaim. Such preachers are ineffective, because they are parochial in outlook. They are trying to tell of a God whose ways are foreign to their own.

The preacher is an ambassador or he is nothing; he represents a Monarch and so his word can only be that which his Monarch commands. His attitudes to men and women must reflect his Monarch's character, and he must walk so humbly that the last word is never his but the Monarch's. And as God is master of the universe the faithful preacher is servant of the whole world.

Paul demonstrated his world-citizenship when he used the word 'ambassador' to describe Christian preachers, for the ambassador is one who is set in one place to serve his Monarch, yet he can only serve him in the one place through knowing the affairs of every place. It is his duty to link places, as well as his own particular place, to the Monarch's court. Empire after empire has, indeed, followed the practice of shifting any ambassador who became too narrowly interested in the one country to which he was sent.

Some might like to think that our Methodist system of itinerating ministers, and planning preachers at many churches, has a similar principle behind it, of which we have seldom thought. Indeed, God has greatly blessed the witness of our Methodist Church whenever we have made this concept of world-embassy our strategy. When we have rebelled against 'our itinerant system' have we done so because we want to nestle into a situation we know well, and can deal with without challenge? When our Societies complain, as at times they have, about the work of a local preacher taking a man away from his own church 'where he could be so useful' just to 'take his sermons round other places' have we forgotten that to preach is to care for a wider world and to speak as ambassadors wherever God sends us?

8. *THE DIPLOMATIC BAG*

Material which others never see gets to ambassadors in the 'diplomatic bag'—a bag of mail which passes censors and Intelligence and comes to the ambassador untouched, straight from his master. So, to lay upon a preacher's shoulders the burdens which we have discussed, without offering him aids, would be grotesque. Where, then, can the preacher find aids to his scrutiny of the world and his interpretation of it?

Little has been said in this discussion about the rôle of the Missionary Society, but it—together with its fellows of the other Churches—is the nerve-centre of our Church's life in the world overseas. The types of problem which we have discussed are the daily concern of men and women whom the Church has set apart to deal with them. The Society sends out a never-ceasing stream of men and women dedicated to the life of the nations and churches to which they are sent. It guides and trains young churches. It watches constantly the changing trends of world affairs, seeking to bring the life of the churches into effective harmony with them. In this process our own and other Missionary Societies amass a great deal of inside information about the way the world's life is going and often the truth of a situation is known in the Mission Houses better than in Fleet Street. (The exposure of the Congo situation by the Baptist Missionary Society is a classic example.) At the same time, by their continual search for suitable candidates for service and their appeals for financial help, the Missionary Societies bring to the rank and file of the Churches the opportunity to get right inside the life of new nations.

The Society of our own Church, therefore, considers it part of its duty to publish both in periodicals and in books the information it has on the meaning of modern history for the Christian Faith. In the *Report of the Connexional Overseas Consultation* and its companion volume, for example, there is a survey of the present world in relation to the life of our churches at home and abroad. In such a periodical as *The Ministers' Missionary Bulletin*—now available to laymen—material is given regularly which should be invaluable to the thoughtful preacher. New experiments with tape-recording have been added to the apparatus for informing the Church of events by commentaries made on the spot overseas. On the great religions of the world the Society's Library can offer sound literature and very extensive files of periodical material. The Society is aware of its duty to help preachers to have a world view.

The Society's servants are constantly out preaching, and would welcome invitations to local conferences of preachers and others who want to gather up-to-date material. District conferences of preachers or leaders will always have priority over other engagements in the Society's diary.

Co-operation is making new sources of material available more and more today. Pre-eminently the *International Review of Missions*, now to be published at Geneva, is a first-rate source of world-cultural material, and the *Ecumenical Press Service*, also coming from Geneva, gives a world symposium of news as it affects the life of the world-Church. Each of the larger Missionary Societies publishes a part of the story of the Church at work. The preacher who is determined to plumb these things for himself can be assured that his Church is with him and will help him to find his way.

Young African and Eastern students come to us after a stay in Britain and tell us that they cannot understand why our people know little geography, and less of current world affairs. They also tell us sadly that they are praying for a revival in the home-land—meaning the United Kingdom. These things make our hearts burn. In many cases we know that these young Methodists are going back to be leaders of nation-building. It is imperative that our people should know and understand the large map on which God is working out His designs. And it is our preachers who must show the way.

NOTE—Some readers may wish to pursue their studies of the literature of other religions (see p. 89). The following are available in the Penguin Classics series: *The Koran*, 5s.; *Buddhist Scriptures*, 3s. 6d.; *Bhagavad Gita*, 2s. 6d.; *Sacred Books of the World* (selections), Bouquet.

The principal work of the Confucian world: *Confucian Analects* (Pub. Pound, 16s.).

Libraries should contain: *The Bible of the World*, edited by Ballou (Pub. Routledge, 50s.).

PART THREE

Biblical Studies

1. Readings in Ezekiel

By the REV. S. CLIVE THEXTON, M.Th.

INTRODUCTION

ON the face of it, the book of *Ezekiel* reveals a much more ordered arrangement and unity than is the case with either of the other two major prophetic books of *Isaiah* or *Jeremiah*.

The opening verses are specific as regards time and place. The date is 593 B.C., and we are introduced to the prophet as one who is '*among the exiles by the river Chebar*' in Babylon. The most natural assumption is that Ezekiel was himself one of the exiles deported from Judah by Nebuchadrezzar in 597 B.C. (see II Kings 24$^{10-17}$), although this is not explicitly stated. At this time the Kingdom of Judah still precariously survived as a puppet state under Babylonian dominance, but was destined to complete eclipse in the destruction of the city and Temple of Jerusalem in 586 B.C. (II Kings 25$^{1-21}$).

Other specific dates are given at various points throughout the book, the last of these (40^1) referring to the year 573 B.C., while the latest in point of time (29^{17}) refers to 571 B.C. While some of the prophet's undated oracles could relate to situations arising after this last date, we are none the less given a clear indication of the main period of his ministry.

After an account of the prophet's vision and call in chaps. 1-3, the main theme of the following chaps. 4-24 is the sure and imminent divine judgement which is to fall upon Jerusalem and Judah. Not only in word, but also in symbolic action (e.g. 4^1-5^{12}, 12$^{1-16}$ etc.), he declares that because of the nation's moral and religious abuses, the Holy City is to fall. In chap. 24 this final disaster is at hand, although the actual fall of the city is not reported until 33^{21}. The intervening chaps. 25-32 are concerned with oracles against Judah's neighbours, who have taken advantage of her plight. They include the magnificent dirge over Tyre in chap. 27, and a forecast of the downfall of Egypt, culminating in the rather macabre passage in which the prophet pictures Pharaoh and his host being welcomed into Sheol, the Hebrew underworld of the dead (32^{17-32}).

The fall of Jerusalem appears to bring Ezekiel some sense of release. The worst has happened, and he can now look forward to the restoration of Israel which he believes God will bring about. This theme of national restoration is the dominant one of chaps. 34–37. The two following chapters contain a difficult passage, apparently foretelling the ultimate overthrow of the gentile nations and the subsequent glorification of the restored Israel. In the final section (chaps. 40–48) we are reminded of Ezekiel's priestly background, for these chapters set out, in considerable detail, plans for the rebuilding of the Temple in Jerusalem, organization of the priesthood and services, and the allocation of tribal boundaries.

This is not the place for any detailed discussion of the problems of *Ezekiel*, which have made the book something of a storm centre of critical discussion for many years. Those interested would do well to read Professor G. W. Anderson's *Critical Introduction to the Old Testament*, pp. 129 ff. Mention may, however, be made of the main questions in dispute:

1. *Is the book the work of a single author?* While many scholars have argued to the contrary, the present tendency is to regard at least chaps. 1–37 as substantially a unity, with the probability that the remaining chapters contain later additions.

2. *Are the dates given in the book reliable?* Partly because the description of the conditions in Jerusalem is very reminiscent of the reign of Manasseh in the first half of the 7th century B.C., some scholars have argued that *Ezekiel* really belongs to that period. Others, however, have gone to the other extreme, and have dated the book in the 4th century B.C., maintaining, for example, that the oracle on Tyre in chaps. 26–28 relates to the siege and capture of Tyre by Alexander the Great. Majority opinion, however, supports the early 6th century dating, as indicated in the book itself.

3. *Did Ezekiel live and work in Babylon, or Palestine, or both?* In chap. 8 we find the prophet describing his 'translation' from Babylon to Jerusalem, from which he returns in 11^{24}. Is this an instance of some form of clairvoyance, or did the prophet some-

how make an actual visit to Palestine? In support of the latter possibility, it is pointed out that his intimate knowledge of the state of affairs in Jerusalem suggests very recent first-hand experience of conditions there. Various alternative suggestions have been made, setting his ministry wholly in Babylon or in Palestine, or as divided between the two.

Whatever the final answer to these questions, it is clear that Ezekiel stands firm in the great tradition of Hebrew prophecy, seeing the course of history governed, not by the whims of chance, but by the will of a sovereign, righteous and merciful God. If his nation is seared by the fires of conquest and destruction, and hammered on the anvil of history, he remains certain that they are the fires of the divine judgement of human sin, and that the anvil is that of the great Master Workman who will bring His work at last to perfect fulfilment. Long before there were any outward signs of the possibility of the return of the exiles to Palestine, and the restoration of the Jewish nation, Ezekiel affirmed his faith in the future, for like the past, it would be the expression of the divine purpose. In a unique way, he is a prophet of striking contrasts, reiterating the insights of those who preceded him, and anticipating those of his successors. No other Old Testament writer has a more vivid concept of the ineffable majesty and transcendence of God, yet none asserts more strongly the inalienable rights and responsibilities of the individual before God. Prophetic preacher *par excellence*, he is none the less loyal to his priestly background in his intense concern for the full restoration of the Temple and cult in the new Israel that is to be. Awakening so many echoes of the earlier prophets, he also, in his mystical symbolic language and descriptions of the portents and glories of the age to come, marks the beginning of that development of apocalyptic literature to become so prominent in the post-exilic age.

In what follows we shall make no attempt to cover the whole book or to deal with all the many aspects of the prophet's message, but only to look at a selection of those passages in *Ezekiel* likely to be of more particular interest to the Christian preacher.

As regards aids to further study, the only small recent commentary is that entitled *Ezekiel, Daniel*, by C. G. Howie, in the S.C.M. Layman's Bible Commentary series. For fuller treatment, the much older *Cambridge Bible* and *Century Bible* are still useful though out of print. The new edition of *Peake's Commentary* will be found helpful here as elsewhere, while those who may have access to it will wish to consult vol. 6 of *The Interpreter's Bible*. For the biblical text itself the *Revised Standard Version* is generally speaking the best to use for study of the Old Testament in English.

CHAPTERS 1–3. THE PROPHET'S VISION AND COMMISSION

Chapter 1. *The Vision of God*

A prophet—or preacher—is, almost by definition, one who has experienced a vision of God. This is not to say that he must necessarily 'see' things unseen, or 'hear' things unheard-of, as Ezekiel did. His vision may come to him through the symbols of worship, as it did for Isaiah, or perhaps even through his seeing a new significance in very ordinary things, as did Jeremiah. Come how it may, the prophet is a man who believes, not as an academic proposition, but because of his own experience of encounter, that God is, and that God speaks His word of blessing or judgement, makes known His own nature and purpose, to those who have ears to hear and eyes to see. So too it is the function of the present day preacher to make his hearers aware that the God of whom he speaks is in truth a living God. This above all is what he is for.

As we read this chapter, we may find ourselves puzzled at many points over the meaning of its details, or may feel it speaks in terms far removed from our own experience, but we are left in no doubt at all by the time we get to the vivid, pulsing climax of the closing verses, that the One who has laid hold of Ezekiel, and set His word upon his lips, is none other than the living God. It is impossible to try to picture in material terms this vision that the prophet describes. Any description of God or of the heavenly realm has to use terms drawn from our dimensions of space and time, for we can only describe the indescribable and unknown in terms of the experienced and known. So we have rather to try to discern the inner or spiritual significance of the terms used, rather than to visualize them pictorially.

We begin with cloud, wind, and fire—symbols of mystery, power, and holiness, and familiar enough to the Hebrew mind as associated with the presence of God. The long description which follows of the four-faced living creatures may, so some suppose, owe a certain amount to the prophet's having subconsciously assimilated something of the religious symbolism of Babylon. However that may be, the cumulative effect of this description is to give a vivid impression of life and movement, of speed and power—all apparently under the absolute control of something or Someone over and above them—in the cloud.

The wheels of verses 15–21 again obviously suggest swift movement, the *'wheel within a wheel'* perhaps indicating circles set in two vertical planes at right angles, suggestive of universality of movement. Those who have any acquaintance with the psychology of Jung will notice the powerful dominance of the concept *'four'* in this passage. There are four living creatures, each with four faces and four wings, four intersecting wheels, and above, the impression of a four-sided platform. To Jung, quaternity or 'fourness' is the symbol of psychic completeness towards which each individual strives. And here in Ezekiel's vision of God there is this same concept of fourfoldness in unity.

There is about this whole passage an overwhelming impression of life and energy. There is *'spirit'* in the wheels, which are in tune with the living creatures, and these latter in turn are in tune with the central intelligence that controls them. This is no cumbersome juggernaut such as featured in the great pagan processions, no sacred idol cart which had to be pushed or pulled along as so much dead weight by a crowd of sweating devotees (cp. Isa. 46^{1-2}). The God of Israel is above all a living God and a mobile God—He can be anywhere in a flash. This sense of the divine mobility or omnipresence was something the exile was to bring home to Israel's faith more vividly than ever before. God was not shut up in a shrine in Jerusalem. He ranged the universe.

Then follows at verse 22 the description of the crystal firmament or platform above the creatures. We recall the significance of this word in Genesis 1^8, *'And God called the firmament Heaven.'* The powerful description of verse 24 adds the imagery of sound to that of sight, thus heightening the over-all impression of splendour and majestic power. Nor is it merely incoherent sound, for from above the firmament there sounds a voice.

From this point—verse 26—as the vision nears its climax, the prophet offers less and less detail and clarity, for He upon whom no man may look and live is beyond human description. But he glimpses a throne. He who rides on the storm is the King of kings. The throne is not clear; it is only something like a throne, of which all earthly thrones are but the merest shadow. And now, at last—the central figure. There is only the suggestion of *'a likeness as it were of a human form'*. The prophet is repudiating the gross animal representations of many of the pagan deities. God is not a superman, but in so far as He bears any likeness to His creatures, the highest of those creatures is the only possible comparison to Him. But from this point all detail is lost in a dazzling blaze of light: '*Such was the appearance of the likeness of the glory of the Lord. And when I saw it, I fell upon my face.*'

> *Who can behold the blazing light?*
> *Who can approach consuming flame?*
> *None but Thy wisdom knows Thy might,*
> *None but Thy word can speak Thy name.*
>
> (ISAAC WATTS, *MHB* 41)

Chapters 2^1–3^{11}. *The Prophet's Commission*

It is interesting to compare the accounts of the call and commission of the three great prophets—Isaiah, Jeremiah, and Ezekiel. When men feel themselves called of God to some great mission, they are frequently carried forward on a wave of conviction and enthusiasm, so that the task before them seems well within their compass. Some disillusionment may come later, but at the beginning no obstacle seems too great to be overcome. Yet in the case of each of these prophets, we find them apparently well aware, right from the start, of the hard and outwardly unrewarding task that lay before them. It may be, as has been suggested, that in the accounts they give us of their call and commission, they are looking back in the light of their subsequent experience, and are saying, 'This is what my commission really meant, even though I did not realize it at the time.' However that may be, we are certainly struck by the rather sombre, indeed almost depressing terms in which their preaching ministry is presented to them. To the young Isaiah, aglow with his vision of the holiness of God—a holiness which has burned out the impurity within his own heart—comes the chilling and almost cynical intimation that the effect of his ministry will be to harden and confirm people in their own spiritual apathy (Isa. 6^{9ff}). The reluctant prophet Jeremiah, shy, sensitive to his youth and inexperience, is brusquely told that he has to bear a message of doom and destruction, and to stand out, isolated and alone, against the rest of his nation (Jer. 1^{4-19}).

So too Ezekiel, staggering to his feet after that overwhelming experience of the splendour and irresistible power of God, is none the less very soon to find that he, as the servant of God, will prove very far from irresistible, but will in fact meet stubborn indifference from those to whom he is sent. None the less, he is not to fear them, for it is of God's word itself that he is possessed (2^8–3^3), and it is this alone that he is to declare, irrespective of his hearers' response to it. There is the hint in 3^{4-7} that God's own people are less responsive to His word than those outside the covenant, perhaps because they have become too familiar with it. But against their stubbornness and hardness of heart the prophet is also to be as hard as flint.

The modern preacher, as much as the prophet of old, will need something of the 'hard-headedness' of Ezekiel. This is not to say that he will always have to preach to indifferent or unresponsive people. There will be many times—perhaps most when least expected—when he will find that his word has struck home to the heart of some hearer, whether to convict, to encourage or to heal. But there will also be many times when there will seem to be no response, when for some reason the great promises and solemn warnings of the Gospel seem strangely devoid of power, and when, as he goes home, the preacher may be tempted to wonder if there was any point in his having preached, or if he is truly called to the work, or even if the Gospel really is the living truth for every man. At such times he needs to remember not only Ezekiel and all the goodly fellowship of the prophets, not even only men of religion, but all those of every faith and of no professed faith, who have stood firm for their convictions, not because they were popular, or because others were impressed by them or accepted them, but because they themselves believed them to be true.

If a man once finds himself, as Ezekiel did, confronted by the living God, if the Gospel of Jesus Christ once lays hold of him, then the fact of God and the fact of Christ become for him the truth, and he must stand firm for it though all the world deny it. And if as part of his personal spiritual experience he has felt the inner compulsion to preach the truth and the word of God, then he cannot easily evade the command to get him to his people and say to them, '*Thus says the Lord God, whether they hear or refuse to hear.*'

Yet if a prophet is a true spokesman of the God who has shown Himself as Reedemer, if a preacher tries to be one of the sheep-dogs of the Good Shepherd, he will not be content with a cold austere 'Take it or leave it.' God Himself might well have said, 'Man has enough light to walk by if only he will be obedient.' In fact, '*God so loved the world that he gave his only Son.*' So the preacher must indeed be hard-headed enough to realize from the outset that his is a tough job, his resolution and perseverance must be like steel, but his heart must be soft, full of the love of God. For it is God's way not to drive, but rather to draw men to Himself. So His spokesman must pray,

> Enlarge, inflame and fill my heart
> With boundless charity divine;
> So shall I all my strength exert,
> And love them with a zeal like Thine;
> And lead them to Thy open side,
> The sheep for whom their Shepherd died.
>
> (CHARLES WESLEY, *MHB* 390.)

Chapter 3[12-27]. *The Watchman of Israel*

However firmly we may lay hold of the truth that religion is not something divorced from life, but must permeate the whole of life, and that we should cultivate a sense of communion with God at all times, it none the less remains that there is still something of a great divide between the time of vision and encounter with God, and the time of service and encounter with the world. Even for Jesus Himself, whose fellowship with His Father was so constant, there had to be the nights of prayer and the times apart. His disciples felt the contrast between being with Him and facing the world, not only on the classic occasion of His transfiguration and its sequel (Mt. 17[1-20]), but on many other occasions. One thinks of Peter's radiant confession of faith and declaration of loyalty in the presence of Christ, and his sad denial of Him before men.

So it is now with Ezekiel. It is still the Spirit of God who takes him to his work and will empower him for it, yet there is also a sense in which his vision of the presence of God fades, and he is left in some sense alone. But the glow of it is with him still, and it is perhaps this that the rather difficult words of verse 14 are intended to convey. The words '*in bitterness*' should in any case probably be omitted, while the following words might be taken in the sense of 'with my soul on fire'. And it is perhaps a true indication of the depth of his feeling, and the reality of this ineffable vision he has experienced, that he cannot glibly or quickly begin to preach, but for a whole week can scarcely begin to think, let alone speak.

It is when he can begin to think that there dawns upon him something of the enormous responsibility that is laid upon him as a preacher. He is like a watchman, upon whose faithfulness and vigilance the lives of many may depend. It would be bad enough if a preacher who failed in his testimony brought only himself under judgement, but unhappily he may well bring many others down with him. The man the prophet fails to warn cannot claim the lack of warning as an excuse. He will suffer the full penalty of his sin. This is because he has other lights to guide and warn him if he will take heed, such as reason, conscience, experience, religion. Even if the prophet had spoken faithfully he might have taken no notice. But on the other hand he might. It is part of the mystery of human freedom that we can never know. Yet we do know that there are many who could say, 'Had it not been for the word that came home to me in such and such a service or meeting, I should have come to a sticky end.' It is a sombre thought that there may be many more, apparently lost for ever from the fellowship of the Church, concerning whom one must always wonder whether, had the word been more faithfully or effectively preached to them, they might not have remained.

Who then will dare to be a preacher? Surely no man, if it were simply a matter of rational, voluntary choice, except perhaps one who had not even begun to see what it really meant. But a man does not 'dare' to preach; he only acknowledges that God has laid hold of him. To whom much is given, of him much is required. He who is granted the vision of God is thereby called to ministry, whether in action, through writing, painting, music—or preaching. There is no discharge in this service. The solitary doctor in a community struck down by cholera must go on until he either conquers the epidemic or dies in the attempt. And the man who has really seen in Christ the place of healing and hope for every man can never excuse himself from the duty of testifying to what he has seen, so long as there are those who need what Christ can give.

After the further vision of God experienced by the prophet (verses 22 ff.) he is told that he will suffer periods of 'dumbness', during which he will be unable to preach. There are other allusions to this later in the book (see 24[27], 33[22]). Some have drawn the conclusion from such references as these that Ezekiel was subject to some kind of nervous disability which sometimes made him literally incapable of speech for a certain period. Others suppose the 'dumbness' relates only to his speaking of the 'word of the Lord'. Whatever may be the truth so far as the prophet is concerned, most preachers know something of this second kind of dumbness, when there seems no insistent word laid upon them, and the question 'What am I to preach about next Sunday?' finds no easy answer. Indeed the preacher may be tempted to wonder whether he is after all called to preach at all, or whether he should give it up. It may be that that question should rather be pondered by the preacher who never suffers from this sense of dumbness rather than by one who does. For while the cause of this experience may be such things as lack of vocation or conviction, failure in prayer, loss of faith and so on, it may also have its root in a healthy and salutary awareness of the heavy responsibility and sometimes almost intolerable burden of preaching. To give it up is superficially the easy way out, though many will know this is impossible for them, and will realize that that searching word of Jeremiah 20[9] is true for them.

What is the preacher to do when, either because of the underlying inner compulsion, or because he is appointed to conduct a certain service, he *must* preach, yet at the same time feels he has nothing to say? Every individual has to find his own answer, and it may be a different answer for each one. One possible way out of this dilemma, when there is apparently no specific message laid upon the preacher, and he feels he has nothing to give, is for him deliberately to choose one of the great central affirmative texts from the New Testament—one which without any doubt contains within it the heart of the Gospel—and to sit down and compel himself to make a sermon upon it, to say as clearly and vividly as he can, what the text says. Very often, if he will do this, his heart and mind will catch fire before he is through. Sometimes he may have to struggle on to the end by force of will alone. However that may be, it is under these conditions that he will very often preach his 'best' sermons, for he will be testifying not to his own bright ideas, or even his own experience, valuable though that may often be, but to the Word of God delivered to him.

CHAPTER 16. THE BRIDE OF GOD

The main burden of chaps. 4–24 is that Judah and Jerusalem stand under the judgement of God because of their disloyalty and sin. The dominant note throughout this section is one of impending doom and stern reproof, tempered here and there by an appeal for penitence, or a glimpse of the ultimate happier future that lies beyond the coming disaster.

The prophet's message in this early phase of his ministry finds vivid and typical expression in the present chapter. He makes use of the bold analogy first used by Hosea (see also Jer. 2^{1-3}, 3^{1-5}, Isa. 50^1) of Israel as the bride of Jahweh. The picture of the unwashed and unwanted female child abandoned by its parents was a familiar enough one in ancient times. It gives vivid expression to Israel's sense of having been adopted by Jahweh, not because of any virtue or value in herself, but by His grace alone, while she was helpless and despised. The classic liturgical confession of this is found in Deuteronomy 26^{5ff}.

This first part of the parable corresponds roughly to the patriarchal period in which, perhaps in the main without her realizing it, Israel was being led towards and prepared for her great destiny. Now at verse 8 we come to what is perhaps the most significant of all the Old Testament words—the word '*covenant*'. Not only does God, as a gracious act of pity, save this people from extinction, but He goes far beyond this, offering her not just His pity, but His love, and committing Himself to her for better for worse, giving her all the material comforts and status of a wife. And while there is no need to press the historical analogy too closely, we are here reminded of the exodus and Mosaic covenant at Sinai, the subsequent conquest of Canaan and eventual achievement by Israel of state and empire under her own king. But all this (verse 14) was still due to God's grace. Israel's very existence as a unit was through the common acknowledgement, by all the constituent tribes, of Jahweh's sovereignty.

But now (verses 15–34) the prophet turns from the divine grace to Israel's response—or lack of response—to it. She who had every reason to be the grateful and loving wife, instead plays the harlot with brazen effrontery. In this long passage, which leaves little to the imagination, the prophet has in mind not only the nation's religious apostasy, by which she betrayed her disloyalty to Him who had given her everything, but also her political opportunism, by which she showed a cynical disbelief in the divine power to conserve that which He had brought into being.

'*Wherefore, O harlot, hear the word of the Lord.*' After the long indictment, now follows the sentence (verses 35–52). Those Israel has dallied with in time past will now lay her low. The penalty prescribed in the Law for adultery was death by stoning (verses 38–40). In the great days of David and Solomon, Israel had been mistress of a Palestinian empire, and most of the neighbouring peoples had suffered at her hands. Ezekiel tells her that now, in the hour of her judgement, they will not pity her, but rather will gloat over her discomfiture, seeking to turn her downfall to their own advantage. For further development of this theme, see 25^2, 26^2, etc.

At this point (verses 44 ff.) the prophet presses home his indictment by reminding Judah that she is one of a bad lot, and that already two of her sisters have suffered for their sins. 'Samaria' stands for the old Northern Kingdom, brought to an end by the Assyrians in 722 B.C., and aptly described as Judah's 'sister' (cp. Jer. 3^{6-9}). The reference to 'Sodom' looks much further back to patriarchal times (Gen. 13^{8-12}, $18^{16}-19^{29}$). The main point the prophet is making is that both to the north and south of Judah there have been in the past signal and terrible instances of the divine judgement, from which she should take warning, instead of which she has outstripped them in wickedness. We note that the supreme sin of which these peoples are held guilty is that of selfish complacency and indifference to the needs of others (verse 49). The inescapable law of human solidarity is one we neglect at our peril, whether as individuals or as nations. The individual who seeks his own ends regardless of other people will in the end reap his reward, if not materially then in spiritual decay and ultimate isolation; for he who lives for himself finishes up in living with himself, which is perhaps as good a definition of hell as any. So too the nation whose actions and policies are governed almost exclusively by national interest, with little or no regard to her responsibilities for less fortunate groups within the human family, will also in the long run suffer a terrible fate, exemplified down the centuries in the awful day of reckoning which the great national and imperial tyrannies have had to face. And in a day and generation when so many nations are so rich, and so many others are relatively so poor, the prophet's warning is a timely one.

Yet for this Old Testament prophet, as well as for a New Testament apostle, 'where sin increased, grace abounded all the more' (Rom. 5^{20}). Even in these earlier years of his ministry, when the burden of his message is of the sure and imminent judgement about to fall upon a sinful nation, Ezekiel is already mindful of the ultimate hope beyond the coming disaster, and it is to this that he turns at verse 53. The hope of the restoration of Samaria as well as of Jerusalem—of Israel as well as Judah—is one he shares with some of the earlier prophets. Jeremiah's great vision of restoration, for instance, includes the old Northern Kingdom as well as the Southern (see esp. Jer. $31^{1-6, 15-22, 31}$). But the promise of a future for Sodom goes beyond this, and implies a hope of a universal redemption. This is particularly characteristic of the three great prophets of the exilic period. We see the expression of hope for the gentile peoples in Jeremiah 12[14-17], 48[47], 49[6, 39], while the second Isaiah goes much further still in his profound conviction that not only are the gentiles to share Israel's redemption, but that she is to be the instrument of their salvation (see esp. Isa. 49[5-6]).

So far as God's own people are concerned, their hope is rooted in the covenant He has made with them and for them (verses 50 ff.). They may break their side of the covenant, but He stands by His side, ever ready to give if they will but receive. It is perhaps hardly necessary to refute the suggestion that this idea of covenant is legalistic. To take the analogy the prophet has himself used in this chapter—that of marriage—we should hardly say that the man who refused to divorce his wife for her unfaithfulness, but remained ready through the years to be a husband to her as soon as she would let him, was simply taking a legalistic attitude. Behind the marriage covenant to which he stands loyal is the love he has for his wife, of which his loyalty is one expression. Even so, as the prophets saw so clearly, behind their covenant was the love of God for His people—unmerited and free—of which His readiness to pledge Himself to her in solemn covenant is one expression. While such a God lived, the prophetic message could never be of unrelieved doom, and while Ezekiel never expresses this sure hope in the love of God in quite such moving terms as do Hosea, Jeremiah and the second Isaiah, there can be no doubt that he shared it, as these closing verses show.

CHAPTER 18. INDIVIDUAL RESPONSIBILITY

We have in this chapter something which, in its general structure, is very much like a sermon. The 'text' is announced in verse 2, but whereas a sermon usually seeks to drive home the truth of the text, here the prophet is concerned rather to refute the proverb he takes as his theme. The greater part of the chapter is then taken up with the application of the proverb to various practical situations, in each of which its inadequacy is affirmed. At verse 25 the argument is summarized and drawn to its conclusion, while from verse 30 to the end the prophet, in true homiletic style, adds his warning and makes his appeal to his hearers or readers.

It need not detract from the importance of Ezekiel's message here, if we acknowledge at the outset the very real fact of that social solidarity of which the proverb speaks. It is true that in ancient Israel this sense of solidarity was much stronger than among most peoples of modern times, and was sometimes applied in a moral and spiritual sense that is quite foreign to our way of thinking. So if one man transgressed some moral or ritual law, a whole community might have to share his liability, as in the familiar story of Achan (Jos. 7). Conversely, if adversity or disaster came upon the social or national group, one tended to look for some individual scapegoat, whose deliberate or unwitting offence was the cause of the trouble. Mention of the scapegoat reminds us that on the positive side, just as individual transgression could involve corporate guilt, so a single or representative act of atonement could bring corporate restoration. The whole cultic system, while certainly providing for individual acts of thanksgiving, penitence or atonement, none the less sought to keep the whole nation right with God by ritual acts performed by one on behalf of all. And finally, there is the explicit declaration (e.g. Exod. 20[5]) that an individual's sin may bring dire consequences, not only upon his contemporaries, but upon generations yet unborn.

The truth underlying all this is that the *consequences* of men's actions do inevitably affect the lives of an incalculable number of other people. We are members one of another. The social and moral environment into which we are born and within which we grow up, formed by the actions and decisions of other people, many of them long dead, is obviously going to affect not only the circumstances of our life, but to some extent the kind of people we shall become. Even Ezekiel's proverb finds grim and almost literal fulfilment in the tragedy of congenital syphilis, one symptom of which may be a jagged malformation of the child's teeth. Here in truth the sins of the fathers—or mothers—are visited upon the children. It is worth observing, however, that this involvement of the many in the actions of the one works both ways. We reap not only the evil consequences of others' folly or wickedness, but also the benefits of others' wisdom, service, and sacrifice. The magnificent work of the long line of social reformers means, so far as this and many other countries are concerned, that the great majority of people have a far better chance of living a decent life, morally as well as materially, than they had a hundred years ago. Or if we lie in hospital suffering from some accident or disease quite clearly caused by the malice or carelessness of another person, it is very likely that we shall be healed by the knowledge handed down by someone who toiled and perhaps suffered to acquire it long ago, of whose existence we may not even be aware.

Yet while recognizing that men suffer the consequences of others' sins, and reap the benefits of others' virtues, what we should want strenuously to deny is that they inherit the *guilt* of those sins—or for that matter acquire the merit of those virtues. So when one man suffers for the sin of another, we should not feel the word 'punishment' to be applicable. Rather should we say that in these and similar instances we reap the consequences of the fact that, for good and evil, we are all bound together in the human family.

Predisposed as we are, however, in all kinds of ways, by the actions and attitudes not only of those about us, but by those of past generations, we yet believe that there is a wide area within which we ourselves are personally responsible people. That a man finishes up as a dustman or a doctor may be due to all sorts of considerations outside his control, but whether he is a good dustman or a good doctor is something for which he is largely responsible. Each man starts his life with certain handicaps or advantages as the case may be, but he incurs neither guilt nor merit from these, but rather from the way in which he rises above his handicaps, or falls below his advantages.

It is this inalienable element of individual responsibility that the prophet is here at pains to stress. We may suppose that in the situation in which he and the other exiles in Babylon found themselves in those dark uncertain years of the 6th century B.C., there was a very strong tendency to lapse into a kind of fatalistic apathy. Disaster had befallen them, disaster of which their prophets had given warning for generations, disaster due to sins of apostasy from their God, and moral failure. But the exiles would believe that the sins for which they now appeared to suffer were not only or even mainly their own, but the sins of their fathers. From this it would be but a short step to the view that it was of little importance whether they themselves were honest or corrupt, moral or immoral, good or bad. The great entail of inherited guilt lay heavy upon them—too heavy to be appreciably increased or reduced by any sin or virtue of theirs.

This moral apathy Ezekiel knows cannot be right, and without necessarily denying the strong element of truth in the corporate view, he strongly affirms that it is not the whole truth. No man, he says, is completely dominated by the past, but is in a real sense the captain of his fate. God deals with men not in the mass, but one by one (verse 4). Then the detailed argument follows. The man who himself lives a good life shall live (verses 5–9), but if his son turns out a bad lot, the latter can take no refuge in his father's virtue, but must bear his guilt (verses 10–13). If in the third generation the grandson of the first man lives a good life, he will not suffer for his father's sins (verses 14–18).

After reiterating the main point of the argument (verses 19–20), the prophet goes on to point out that a man is not only responsible for his fate, but remains responsible throughout his life. The man who after an evil life sincerely repents will find forgiveness, while the good man who falls into evil ways will not be saved by his earlier virtue (verses 21–28). One is reminded of Bunyan's warning in his *Pilgrim's Progress*, that even from the gate of heaven there is a way to hell.

What are we to understand of the promise that the righteous man shall '*live*', or the warning that the wicked man will '*die*'? Certainly up to the time of the exile, Hebrew thought gave little place to the concept of life after death. There was some kind of existence beyond the grave, but it was only a poor shadow of mortal life itself. Hence it was believed that a man's destiny was fulfilled in this life. If he did right, he could expect prosperity and long life; if he did evil, he might look for adversity, sickness and a premature death. On this view one could reconcile apparently innocent suffering with the divine justice only by supposing the sufferer to be less innocent than he appeared—a supposition which forms the recurring theme in the argument of Job's friends. Similarly with the case of the prosperous rogue, if God was just, one could only assume that some really terrible fate awaited such a man, which would cancel out the blessings he had received. This traditional view was clearly doomed to dissolution. The exilic period in which Ezekiel lived, and more particularly the years of frustration and disappointment which followed the exile, saw that dissolution taking place. It became abundantly clear that for very many the divine justice was not vindicated in this life. There were two possible reactions. One was to abandon belief in a just, righteous and omnipotent God altogether. To the Hebrew mind this was unthinkable. The other alternative was to suppose that death was not the end of the story, and that the real *dénouement* of life lay beyond the grave. It was this supposition that was to grow, during the last centuries of the pre-Christian era, into a positive hope, a hope which for the Christian is made sure and certain by the resurrection and ascension of Jesus Christ. Standing on its own, His shameful death—the death of the righteous, innocent man after a blameless life of service and sacrifice—would have been a blatant denial of the old philosophy, and a declaration either that God did not care or that, if He did, He could do nothing. But Christ's triumph beyond death, evidenced not only by the resurrection stories but by the whole growth and survival of the Church through the ensuing years, demonstrates that the last word is with God, and that that word is spoken not here, but hereafter.

To what extent, if any, this hope burned in the mind of Ezekiel, nearly six hundred years before the birth of Christ, we cannot tell. What we can say is that he had a very firm grasp of some of the premises upon which the great conclusion of the Christian hope was to stand. He has within him the grass roots of the evangelical faith: that every man has the right and responsibility to stand before God on his own account; that no man can rely on his father's virtue or need bear the guilt of his father's sin; that repentance will always be met by the divine forgiveness; that because there always lies before men the choice of the two ways, preaching is literally a matter of life and death.

So it is that in the closing verses (29–32) the prophet makes his appeal. It is an appeal to his hearers to turn from sin to God, from the way of destruction to the way of life. Although in one sense a man cannot make for himself '*a new heart and a new spirit*', yet as soon as he truly and decisively turns from evil and puts himself into the hand of God, then from that moment he does become a new creature, his attitudes and responses hardly recognizable to those who knew him before. It is this deep inner transformation, wrought only by the Holy Spirit, that God longs to bring about in every man who will consent to it, for it is not His will that one of His children should perish. So far from that, the Cross of Jesus stands as perpetual reminder of how deep is His concern that instead, they should have everlasting life.

This vivid passage, as we should expect, was not missed by Charles Wesley, and in the second verse of his hymn based upon it, he adds to Ezekiel's phrase the searching appeal of the Cross:

> *Sinners turn; why will ye die?*
> *God, your Saviour, asks you why:*
> *God, who did your souls retrieve,*
> *Died Himself, that you might live.*

(*MHB* 327)

CHAPTER 34. THE SHEPHERD OF ISRAEL

Here is one of those Old Testament passages in which, with almost uncanny insight, the writer discerns the shape of things to come. Its vivid anticipation of the incarnation of God in Jesus Christ would make it in some ways a far more appropriate Christmas Old Testament reading than many of those traditionally used. This is not because the writer sees the future in any clairvoyant sense, but because he sees deeply into the nature of God, whose redemptive concern for His people will not for ever tolerate the failure of His human instruments to do His will.

We cannot be precise regarding the identity of the '*shepherds*' of verses 1–10. The term is used here, as elsewhere in the Old Testament, of civil or national leaders. If this chapter is to be ascribed to Ezekiel himself, then we must assume he is referring to the kings and their governments who ruled in Jerusalem until its destruction by Babylon in 586 B.C. After the death of good king Josiah in 608, Judah was ruled by a series of puppet kings whose incompetence and foolish attempts at rebellion brought their people at last to disaster, news of which soon reached those already in exile (see 33^{21}), and must have seemed to many of them to mean the final extinction of any lingering hope they may have cherished. The prophet Jeremiah, who was in Jerusalem during those terrible last years, also had some scathing things to say about these '*shepherds*' (see Jer. 22 and 23^{1-6}, the latter passage being very similar to the present chapter).

Many scholars would, however, assign a later date to this chapter than that of Ezekiel himself, in which case we must regard a later editor as its author. It has been maintained that the diction and vivid picture of the Davidic Messiah are suggestive of a post-exilic date. In this case we must identify the '*shepherds*' with the leaders of the restored community in Palestine during the frustrating and disappointing years of the late 6th and early 5th centuries B.C. Another prophet, probably of that period, also has some hard things to say of the leaders of his time (Isa. 56^{9-12}).

Whether we ascribe these words to Ezekiel himself or not, there is no doubt that they faithfully reflect what we noted earlier, that when news of the fall of Jerusalem came, so far from losing hope, he now felt able to look forward beyond present distress to a future hope which relied, not on human power, but on the power of God. Nor do problems of authorship and date alter the abiding truths contained in these verses.

The indictment of verses 1–10 is directed against those who exploit the privileges of their leadership, but ignore its responsibilities. To Hebrew thought there was only one authority—that of God. The authority of their kings was not that of a man, but of a human instrument endued with the Spirit of God conveyed to him through the oil of his anointing. Although there were those who regarded the monarchy as a denial of theocracy, others saw it as the human means through which the rule of God could find expression. Any ruler, therefore, who showed himself to be acting contrary to the divine will, had not authority, and would surely fall. Conversely, any ruler, even though not a worshipper of the God of Israel, who none the less showed he had authority by his success in rule or conquest, must have in some sense the authority of God. Hence the first Isaiah can hail Assyria as the 'rod' of God's anger (Isa. 10[5]), while the second Isaiah can term Cyrus God's 'messiah' or 'shepherd' (Isa. 44[28], 45[1]).

Since God has shown in so many ways His concern for the true welfare of His children, the writer is sure that these rulers of whom he speaks, who have no concern for people, are without true authority and will be swept away. They are not faithfully representing Him whose servants they are supposed to be.

These searching words need to be pondered, not only by civil or temporal rulers, but by all who wield any kind of influence or authority over other people. People belong to God, and what power we may hold over them is not for our benefit but for theirs. What is said here is addressed to politicians whose main concern is party or personal advantage, to ministers who have forgotten their pastoral office, to teachers and parents whose dealings with their children are governed more by their own pride than by a genuine love for the children, to leaders in commerce and industry who put profits above people, to writers and speakers who propagate popular falsehood rather than hard truth, and to a host of others. For all these are 'shepherds', with a responsibility to those who look to them for guidance.

Nor do these words come home only to individuals, but to groups and communities as well. The leaders of a local church might do well to spend time going through these verses and asking themselves how true a shepherd their church is in its neighbourhood. Our whole system of government, and in particular our social services, may be called in question if they fail to care adequately for people, and especially for those who, through youth or age, sickness or adversity, cannot care for themselves.

And so to the tremendous '*I myself*' of verses 11–16. One might almost, without irreverence, speak here of the 'impatience' of God. His creation of man as a being with freedom of choice, with the power to make or mar his destiny, involved God's self-limitation of His own authority. Like the parent who knows his child must 'do it himself' if he is to grow up, God delegates to man a good deal of the direction of his own affairs. And if we take seriously the thought that God loves men and women, we can very faintly imagine something of the anguish that this restraint must involve for God. One gets a glimpse of this anguish through a passage such as Hosea 11, or parts of Jeremiah, and in the wistful lament of Jesus, '*O Jerusalem . . . how often would I . . . and you would not*' (Lk. 13[34]). How long can God stand by while men, through their own folly or self-will, ignore the light they have and instead choose darkness, setting not only their own feet on the way of destruction, but the feet of many others misled by their example?

The answer of the prophets is 'Not for ever'. Sometimes they think of the course of history itself conspiring to bring about a new conformity to the divine will. At others they envisage a mighty cataclysmic intervention by God which will smash the forces of evil and bring to summary judgement all those men who are in rebellion against Him. But running through the prophecies is a thread of clear gold, of which the present passage is a shining strand, which sees the ultimate divine intervention not as the summary edict of some remote Controller of Destiny, but as the costly involvement of God Himself, not over and above, but rather within the framework of that which man has been called to do and be. So the divine answer to the failure of the unscrupulous human shepherds of Israel is to say, '*I myself will be the shepherd of my sheep*'.

The prophet never saw the fulfilment of his words, but when at last the redemptive love of God broke through in the Incarnation, He who came was One who called Himself '*the Good Shepherd*'. Not only in the days of His flesh, but through all the centuries since, He has been seeking out His sheep. Yet the miracle is that although God Himself comes to man in Jesus, He does so in such a way that human freedom is not overruled. He who is Lord and Master none the less comes to men as their Servant. They can gladly receive what He offers to do for them, or turn their back on Him. They can follow Him or crucify Him.

This analogy of the Shepherd of Israel runs right through the

Bible. Jeremiah uses it (31^{10}), as does the second Isaiah (40^{11}), while it features in a number of psalms (e.g. 23, 80, 95^7). Its appearance in the New Testament centres on the familiar John 10, while later writers remind us of it again (Heb. 13^{20}, I Pet. 2^{25}). Of the many Christian hymns on this theme two of Charles Wesley's draw us very close to the heart of personal faith in Christ—'*Jesus the good Shepherd is*' and '*Thou Shepherd of Israel, and mine*' (*MHB* 621 and 457).

The remainder of the chapter, verses 17–34, has all the main features of Messianic prophecy. Many who attribute the first part of the chapter to Ezekiel himself, none the less believe these verses to be a later addition, expressive of the post-exilic Messianic hope. There is to be salvation or vindication for the poor and helpless, while the aggressive and unscrupulous are to be subdued. A ruler of David's line will bring in an age of justice and peace, while the very course of nature will conspire to ensure unprecedented prosperity. The people of God will no longer be a prey to tyrants, but will dwell securely, '*and none shall make them afraid*'.

We may question what we may regard as the somewhat materialist expression of this hope, but the reality of the hope depends not upon men's imperfect visions of what it implies, but upon the nature of God. If God is One who really cares for those He has set within this mortal life for the very purpose that through it they may receive power to become His children, then for those who seek that purpose there is a sure and certain hope. The writer of these words believes in such a God, who says to His people, '*You are my sheep, the sheep of my pasture, and I am your God.*'

CHAPTER 37^{1-14}. GOD AND THE IMPOSSIBLE

Though perhaps the one really familiar passage in Ezekiel for many, this vision of the dry bones well repays repeated pondering, and the message it carries is above all a message for preachers.

We cannot know just how we are to take these verses in so far as the prophet's own situation is concerned. Was it indeed a vision, discerned in one of those strange trance states to which he seems to have been prone? Or is he making up this powerful allegory as a means of bringing home to his hearers his deep conviction that, in spite of everything, Israel will live again? Certainly it must have been no easy conviction to convey to others, for if, as we may suppose, the prophet is speaking about 580 B.C., it was at a time when national hopes were almost extinct. The fall of Jerusalem in 586 to Babylon, involving the destruction of the Temple and the end of the Kingdom of Judah, would still hold its crushing effect on the minds of the exiles. The rise of Persia, through whom restoration was to become possible, and which animated the hopes of the second Isaiah, was not yet. Babylon ruled as the dominant world power, and humanly speaking the future held no hope for her subject peoples. All this is vividly conveyed in verse 11 of this chapter. Of the vital, pulsing life the people of God had once known, there seems nothing left but dry bones whitening under the sun, mute and macabre relics of what had once been a mighty host.

We may suppose that the question with which the prophet had to wrestle in his own heart and mind is the one contained in verse 3—'*Son of man, can these bones live?*' His answer, that only God knows, is the right one, for it is the answer of faith. In our own time the phrase 'God knows' is a profane and flippant way of saying that nobody knows, but here it is very much more than that. If in answer to the question the prophet boldly says, 'Yes, they can', then he is presuming too far, for certainly no human power can make this happen, and if the death of the nation is due, as he has himself so often declared, to her sin and apostasy, there would seem no reason to expect a miracle. If on the other hand he replies, 'No, they cannot', he is not only setting a limit to both the power and the grace of God, but he is also allowing himself to sink into the despair and unbelief of those to whom he is called to speak. To reply '*O Lord God, thou knowest*', is the right answer, because it recognizes the divine wisdom and power on the one hand, but recognizes too that the course of events is always determined to some extent by the exercise not only of God's sovereignty, but also of that delegated sovereignty which He has given to man. What may be God's will does not necessarily happen unless it also gains the support of some human wills—perhaps only one man's will. Yet where even one man is prepared humbly to acknowledge what the power and grace of God may do, and thereby to offer himself as the human partner of God's work, then the impossible can happen. And this surely is what the Bible is about. Moses, Elijah, Isaiah, Jeremiah—all these and many others provide as it were a bridgehead for the divine activity, the human response—however hesitant or imperfect—which God seeks before His redemptive work can be carried forward. Now, it is, so far as we know, yet again one man who is able to make this response of faith, and to say quietly and with full sincerity, '*Thou knowest.*'

And immediately, in verse 4 there comes the reply, 'If you really believe it depends on Me, then I tell you that it also depends on you. *Prophesy to these bones.*' We are reminded again of Moses pleading with God to save his people from bondage in Egypt, suddenly taken aback by the fact that God accepts the faith implied in his request, and says, '*Come, I will send you to Pharaoh*' (Exod. 3[10]). So now to Ezekiel, 'You say that these bones might live by my word. Very well, I give you my word. Proclaim it—to these bones!'

Perhaps the most significant words in the passage are those of verses 7 and 10: '*So I prophesied, as I was commanded*'—and it happened! How absurd, to preach to bones, to preach to the wind! But the prophet does as he is told. He does not know what may come of it, or whether anything may come of it, but he believes that 'God knows', and is prepared to leave the issue to the divine knowledge and power.

To Ezekiel this is perhaps a dream or vision, but to the modern preacher very much of a reality. While there are many places in which he is appointed to preach, where there is plenty of evidence of vitality and hope, there are many more where there seems little of either. As he faces that almost empty building, or that ugly little box of a place, or that tiny group of familiar faces; as he goes to preach the word of God in churches which humanly speaking have been dead for years, what is he to say to the questions of this chapter? Can these bones live? Can the cleansing, searching wind of the Spirit blow through this dusty, stagnant place? The 'No' of the preacher who in his heart has given up hope of anything happening is perhaps not much more useless than the over-confident but superficial 'Yes' of the man who glibly recites the well-worn 'Revival can happen here' sermon he has been taking round for the past ten years. The plain fact is that the preacher never knows the answer, but he must cling to the belief that God does know. As he goes into the pulpit he must try to remember that for reasons he does not and need not know, the grace of God can awaken a new and vital response in the heart of one or more of those present, a response from which perhaps tremendous consequences may flow. But it is for him, the preacher, to provide the link. If he fails, then that which God knows *can* happen perhaps will not happen.

This may seem too heavy a responsibility for him to bear (see above on 3^{12-27}), but only as the preacher tries somehow to bear it will he preach, not his own word but the word of God. Only so will he be prepared, in contradiction of every apparent probability, to preach none the less to dry bones, or to preach to the wind. God, he believes, may know that today the dead will come to life, or the tide of the Spirit come flooding in.

Ezekiel did not live to see the day of restoration of which he dreamed, but he lived and preached as one who never failed to believe that at any moment God may know that the impossible can happen, and that, given only the faithful witness to His word of grace, it may awaken a response in those who hear it. '*So I prophesied as he commanded me, and the breath came into them, and they lived.*'

CHAPTER 47¹⁻¹². THE RIVER OF LIFE

Ezekiel's hope for the future included not only the restoration of political independence under a new and greater king of David's line, not only the overthrow of the great gentile powers who had so often harassed and ravaged Israel in the past, not only the rebuilding of the Holy City, but the restoration to its full splendour and majesty of the Temple itself and its sacred ritual. It is this cultic restoration that he envisages in great detail in chaps. 40–46.

This is perhaps only to be expected of one who, in the opening verses of the book, is described as '*Ezekiel the priest*'. Yet this emphasis on the central importance of the Temple and its cultus is not unique to Ezekiel, but is one of the central themes of post-exilic prophecy. This may seem a little strange if we turn our minds back to the great figures of the 8th and 7th centuries B.C. Amos and Isaiah describe the religious ritual of their day in scathing terms (e.g. Amos $5^{21\text{ff}}$, Isa. $1^{10\text{ff}}$), while Jeremiah even prophesies the destruction of the Temple itself (Jer. 7^{1-15}). We need not, however, assume that these prophets condemned all religious ritual as such, but only that of their own time in so far as it had become mere empty form. In a time of great material prosperity they condemned the complacent, formal observance of ritual as something which blinded men's eyes to the need for that justice and righteousness God really required from them. Yet after the exile the pendulum swung right over; and, in a day of material poverty and depression, prophets like Haggai, Zechariah, and Malachi declare that until and unless the cult is worthily restored and sustained, nothing else in the national life will go right.

There is no necessary contradiction between these two points of view. It is true that a religion which contents itself with formal acts, but is unconcerned with morality or social justice, is to be condemned. It is also true that when religion becomes almost identified with social service, it quickly degenerates into mere humanitarianism, with little reference, beyond human enlightenment or expediency, to that absolute demand and offer which men encounter in their worship of the living God. What is needed, therefore, is the kind of worship that, so far from being a mere formality, vividly and constantly affirms the great truths about God and man, about life and destiny, that these may inform and guide every human activity and relationship.

So then, at the centre of his restored nation that is to be, Ezekiel sees a restored Temple and ritual. It was for a Christian visionary, writing some 650 years later, to go beyond this, and to say of the ultimate City of God, 'And I saw no temple therein' (Rev. 21^{22}). For him, the presence of God would in Heaven be so clear and pervasive that no particular place would be set apart for worship. Everywhere would be the temple of God, and every activity an act of worship. Yet there is a real sense in which Ezekiel, in this vision of his, anticipates this. He still envisages a temple, marked off from its surroundings, but he sees too (like the builders of Coventry Cathedral) that that for which it stands cannot be confined within it, but must flow from it, and so pervade everything that all may be restored to the perfect harmony of the divine rule.

This thought is expressed by the picture of the water flowing from the threshold of the Temple, increasing in volume until it becomes 'a river that could not be passed through' (verse 5). It becomes, as indeed does any river in a dry land, a river of life. Trees clothe its banks, fish swarm in its depths. Most significant of all, it flows from Jerusalem away to the east (verse 8), down into the deep cleft of the Jordan valley, down to where, some 1,300 feet below the level of the Mediterranean, lie the thick, salty, stagnant, lifeless waters of the Dead Sea. Into *this* sea the river of life flows, and the waters are 'healed'.

Here surely is a great parable of the mission of the Church. For this is the function of the Church, so to receive through its worship and prayer and sacraments the very life and power of

God, that from it there may go out a life-giving stream to heal the waters of the dead sea which is the world.

Perhaps it may seem that the modern world, with its restless turmoil, its vast and precariously restrained energies, its social and political ferment, its march towards new heights of material achievement, is very far from being dead, whatever else it may be. Yet it remains true that the scent of death hangs heavy upon it, not only because of man's terrible nuclear power of self-destruction, but because all human life and activity which leaves out of account that vertical dimension which only faith and worship can give, gives rise in the long run to a sense of futility and emptiness.

Nor is this vision of the life-giving stream flowing from the Church to the world to be dismissed as mere wishful thinking. It is not only a hope for the future, but a fact of the past, that through the centuries the Church of Christ has brought life and light to countless places, people, and social situations where before was only darkness and death. Its work and witness have only too often been shadowed by the pride or folly of those within it, yet when one remembers that work, not only in missionary enterprise, but in all kinds of social and redemptive work, and above all through the life and influence of its members, one realizes how rich a source of new life it has been.

We take our leave of Ezekiel as he looks forward into the unknown future at a time when outwardly only the ruins of his nation's life remain, yet when he sees none the less a sure and certain hope. Beyond present troubles he sees the day of restoration, when the people of God, no longer dispossessed, scattered, and broken, will once more dwell in their own land around the Holy City, from whose Holy Place the healing, renewing power of their God will stream forth to make their land yet again as the Garden of Eden.

The Christian, while also believing that he is called to play his part in helping to carry the light and truth of God into every part of life and society, and that in this work he must spend and be spent, none the less does not look for its full realization here, but hereafter. Like Ezekiel, he too looks for the City of God, no longer ravaged and marred by sin and mortality, but fair and splendid as the seer of Patmos saw her, '*coming down out of heaven from God, made ready as a bride adorned for her husband*' (Rev. 21[2]). And it is there, in that eternal city God has prepared for those who confess they are strangers and pilgrims on the earth, that there flow the healing waters once glimpsed long ago by a lonely prophet in Babylon. '*Then he showed me the river of the water of life, bright as crystal, flowing from the throne of God and of the Lamb through the middle of the street of the city* (Rev. 22[11]).

2. Glimpses of the Life of Jesus (Part Two[1])

By the REV. DR J. ALEX FINDLAY, M.A.

VII. ENCOUNTERS WITH THE GENTILES

IT is usually taken for granted that our Lord's sole purpose in His long journey through Syria and the Lebanon was the training of the twelve; and that was undoubtedly His primary motive. But the chapters in Mk 7[24]–10[31] which tell us of His travels are as much concerned with crowds and encounters with the Pharisees on the one hand, and with the sick on the other; and Matthew makes it still clearer that Jesus was not by any means in solitary retreat with His twelve. His desire for secrecy is evident in Mk 7[24], but it is clear that it was disappointed.

The story of the Syro-Phoenician woman and Jesus' whimsical reply to her call for help, 'Let the children have their supper first; it is not right to take the children's bread and give it to the puppy-dogs' and the additional sentence in Matthew, 'I was not sent except to the lost sheep of the house of Israel' (which might mean 'to these sheep lost from the house of Israel' and taken this way, implies a rebuke to the twelve for wishing to send the woman away) might leave a nasty taste in our mouths, but for the fact that puppies are treated as household pets in Palestine and Syria; in fact children were called 'puppies' (cp. our kiddies?). It is only right, Jesus suggests, that the children should get their supper first; the puppy-dogs under the table will get their turn. The woman was not insulted, and she answers wittily, and by her wit she gets what she wants. In Matthew Jesus' praise for a woman who dared to answer Him back, and in His own coin, is even greater ('O woman, great is thy faith') and according to Mark He says, 'Because of that word you may go home, the demon is gone out of your daughter.' We are reminded of the gentile soldier of whom Jesus said, 'I have not found so great faith, no not in Israel.'

He left Tyre and passed through Sidon to the eastern side of the Lake of Galilee; in that short phrase is summarized a journey that would take some days; the direct way of going to Decapolis

[1] This was the last thing Dr Findlay wrote before his death; and he wrote it specially for *The Preacher's Handbook*. Part One appeared in *Number Seven* of this series.

would have been back to Galilee, and across the water, but the phrase 'through Sidon' means that for the time being Jesus and His twelve are avoiding going into Galilee. The only thing we are told about this journey over the slopes of Lebanon is the story of the man with an impediment in his speech. The most significant feature in this narrative is the fact that Jesus takes the man 'away from the crowd' and uses saliva. The man is a gentile, there is a language difficulty. It was generally believed that saliva—especially the saliva of a holy man—had healing properties. Jesus finds it difficult to make contact with the man, and using His own Aramaic He says 'ephphatha' (Be thou opened). He looks up to heaven, sighing as He does so. The cure was complete but, as in Galilee, it brought the crowd together and made futile all His endeavours to keep people from talking about Him.

The really important thing about the second miraculous supper is that it is not a mere replica of the first. The language is slightly more sacramental, and the additional information that the crowd had been in attendance on Him for three days is of importance; they are far from home. Generally, scholars have been inclined to regard this as simply an alternative version of the first story. Luke ignores it, but Matthew follows Mark and introduces it with a lyrical account of the rapturous delight of the crowd, and a very remarkable addition: 'They glorified the God of Israel' (Mt. 15^{31}). This would be a mere commonplace were the crowd not a Gentile crowd; but that being so, it becomes full of significance. All that we need say is that, if it was a crowd largely composed of Gentiles with whom Jesus entered into sacramental fellowship, the story is very relevant.

In any case, Jesus' old enemies, the Pharisees, tracked Him down here, and met Him with a new challenge. Let Him give them a 'sign from Heaven'—a clap of thunder would do. Their phrase for a sign from heaven is 'Bath Qol'—that is, daughter of the Voice (of God). We remember how the people of Jerusalem said 'that was a clap of thunder', others said 'an anger spoke to Him' (Bath Qol) when the voice from heaven spoke to Jesus (Jn 12$^{28, 29}$). Again Jesus sighed, and told them no sign was to be given to this generation; Matthew adds 'except the sign of the prophet Jonah'—which could be a mistake for 'the sign of John' (the Baptist) (12^{39}, cp. Lk. 11^{29}). The names Jonah and John are often confused in MSS. (cp. Mt. 16^{17} with Jn 1^{42}).

Once more Jesus had to get away from His persecutors by getting into a boat, but this time He took the twelve with Him.

In their hurry they had neglected to take food with them and they were disturbed about this. Jesus tells them that they should not have forgotten so soon about the miraculous supper parties by the lake. Meanwhile the Pharisees were intriguing with Herod's friends to get rid of Him; they had better have nothing more to do with these people but rather leave them to themselves. Weeks before He had told them that it was given to them to see 'the mystery of the Kingdom of God'. Other people had eyes, but could not see; but blessed were their eyes that were given such sights to see. Now He has to say to them, 'Why can't you see what is going on under your eyes?' (Mt. 13[16]).

When they landed at Bethsaida some of them were on familiar ground. There was still need for secrecy, for Jesus had been there before. A blind man is brought to Him, and once again He uses saliva in the healing. Jesus takes him outside the town. At first the man looks away into the distance when Jesus touches him, and says he can see what he takes to be men—because they are moving about—but they look to him like trees. When Jesus touches him again, his sight is fully restored, and he sees everything (or 'every one') clearly. None of the gospel stories is so obviously an acted parable as this. I am surprised that I have never heard a sermon about it; it is really asking to be preached about. For the whole section of Mark's gospel in which this story is found is concerned with the blindness of the twelve. Jesus had 'taken them for a walk' away from friends and home. For them it is a walk in the dark, but at the touch of their Leader they are gradually beginning to see. Their new vision is not yet adjusted to the new world which Jesus calls the Kingdom of God; but it will not be long now before the Kingdom of God will dawn upon them, in all its power and glory.

So, after Jesus' flying visit to Bethsaida, they set out for Caesarea Philippi. He is now leaving the dominion of Herod Antipas for that of Herod's brother Philip. By and by, after following the course of the river for some time, they enter a wooded glen; and this brings them to the foot of a rock, a famous spot where two religions meet—the worship of the emperor, enshrined in the temple on the rock which was dedicated to Caesar, and an allegedly unfathomable grotto beneath, sacred to Pan, where from times immemorial the nature-gods of paganism had been worshipped. And now a third religion has come upon the scene with this group of the disciples of Jesus. He has already asked them what people are saying of Him; now He asks them,

'What do you say about Me?' Peter answers for them all, 'Thou art the Christ.' Luke has 'the Christ of God', Matthew 'the Christ, Son of the Living God' (Lk. 9^{20}, Mt. 16^{17}). The praise given to Peter's confession is peculiar to Matthew's gospel.

It is strange that Jesus receives the statement with nothing but a strong warning that they are to keep it to themselves for the time being, following this up with the first prophecy of his own death and resurrection. The really important thing is the substitution for 'the Christ' of 'the Son of Man'. Did Jesus dislike the idea of Messiahship, only accepting the title 'Christ' with reluctance? It is tempting to think so. If so, the Church has always called Him by a name which He rarely, if ever, used for Himself. We shall see later that even when He stood before the High Priest, it is questionable whether Jesus really accepted this title.

In Palestine Messiahship was hopelessly entangled with the idea of a holy war with Rome, and Luke's Gospel makes it clear that Jesus was intensely conscious at that time of the danger of a war which could only have one ending. Public indignation was rising against Pilate and Herod, and Jesus fought against the idea of revolt and the pressure that would have made Him its leader. Words like, 'Except ye repent, ye shall all likewise perish' (Lk. 13^{1-3}) should not be interpreted, as they often are, as referring to the fate of sinners in general, but to the doom of those who persisted in revolt against Rome, and this too is the meaning of 'Resist not him that is evil'. But there was more to His preference for the term 'Son of Man' than that. The key to this mystery is the challenge about cross-bearing which follows. True conquest will come, not in the world's way, but through suffering.

When Peter makes his protest against the shocking disclosure of the future prospects of the 'Son of Man' he is sharply rebuked. We need not worry about the fact that he is addressed as 'Satan'; Matthew makes it clear that the word is not a proper name in this passage, though its use here does remind us of the Temptation scene. 'Out of my way; you are a hindrance to me!' (Mt. 16^{23}). Though Peter had flashes of insight, he was still living in one world, and Jesus in another. To make it quite clear that He is not thinking of Peter only, Jesus addresses the crowd, along with the twelve, and tells them that anyone who wishes to be a follower of His must be ready to go with Him wherever He leads, even to martyrdom; their souls are at stake, as well as His. Seeing their downcast looks, He promises them that some of those standing around Him will live to see the Kingdom of God upon earth.

It was only a week later that Jesus took Peter, James, and John up the slopes of Mount Hermon, which overlooks Caesarea Philippi. They may have spent the night at snow level. With the morning sun on the mountain snow they see their Master with His face shining like the sun, and His garments whiter than the snow; and there are two men with Him, about both of whom they have been thinking lately. One was Moses, whom God had buried and no one knew where; and the other was Elijah, who had been taken up to Heaven in a chariot of fire. Moses had fed the crowd, as Jesus had done so recently, with manna from Heaven; and Elijah was expected to come again to anoint the Messiah. It was believed that a prophet like Moses would appear—as the first sign that the consummation was at hand—and lead God's people away from their oppressors into the desert, and feed them with heavenly manna; and then Elijah was to appear and anoint one of them—some said a son of David, from Bethlehem—to lead them against their enemies and set up the Kingdom of God in Jerusalem.

Each of the first three evangelists has his own story of what the three disciples saw on this never-to-be-forgotten morning. Luke suggests that as Jesus prayed the appearance of His face changed; Mark stresses the fear of the three watchers, and Peter's suggestion that he should make three shrines to worship these three; both Mark and Matthew bring out that Moses and Elijah fade away into the mist and that the disciples are left alone with Jesus. All make it clear that the vision was a great experience for the disciples. On the way down the mountain, they are charged to keep the vision secret till 'the Son of Man is risen from the dead'.

When they get back to the others, they find a confused and painful scene. A man has come with his epileptic son, and has asked to see Jesus. The remaining disciples, not knowing when He will be back, have tried to help but in vain. Unfortunately their old enemies the Scribes have also arrived on the scene, and are eagerly making capital out of their embarrassment. They have been watching for the return of the Master, whilst trying to conciliate the exasperated father; and their position has become almost desperate when at last Jesus appears. The man approaches Him without any respect and pours out his complaint. To make matters worse the boy has another fit, and the father cries, almost in despair, 'If thou canst do anything, have compassion on us and help us' (Mk 8[22]).

Jesus immediately reacts to the word 'if'. On another occasion a leper had said 'If thou wilt'; here the man says 'If thou canst'. One doubts His will, the other His power. In both cases Jesus protests, 'You say "if" to Me; I say it all depends on you. All things can be, if you believe.' Immediately the man cries out, 'Sir, I believe; help me out with my unbelief.' By this time a crowd is coming together and Jesus hastens to deal with the case. It is difficult, but it is done. When the disciples ask why they failed, Jesus tells them that difficult cases like this cannot be undertaken offhand. Here Matthew puts in a saying (Mt. 17¹⁶) about the faith which moves mountains. As there was actually a mountain between Jesus and His disciples that morning, this word was indeed appropriate.

One cannot help feeling that Jesus was not satisfied with some at least of the twelve at this stage. His choice of only three of them to witness His transfiguration is suggestive. Amongst those who were left a discussion was going on on the subject of leadership. Evidently there was some jealousy of Peter's position, for he has reason for complaining of a 'brother' sinning against him (Mt. 18²¹). He does not say who the offender is but behind the general question there generally lurks a practical difficulty. Was Judas Iscariot the offending person? Again in Matthew there is a parable (Mt. 20¹ff) about labourers in a vineyard who are jealous because they, who have borne the 'burden and heat of the day' have been put on a level with men who have only worked one hour. There is good reason for the belief that Judas had been with Jesus from the beginning of His ministry; in several places he is called 'the one of the twelve' which means 'the first of the twelve'. He was the man whom Jesus called 'comrade' (Mt. 26⁵⁰). Peter had been with Jesus a comparatively short time, yet he had been called the rock on which the new synagogue was to be built. Jesus often said, 'The first shall be last and the last first.' Was this principle being illustrated in the circle of His innermost friends?

John, the son of Zebedee, has found someone who does not belong to their company, using the name of Jesus to cast out demons, and has protested. But he need not do so, Jesus explains; anybody who uses His Name in doing something great is a friend of His.

The incident of the children being brought to Jesus and His obvious affection for them is always specially appealing to us. Why did the twelve try to keep them away? Jewish children are often spoilt (I found them very obtrusive and difficult to restrain, in Galilee); and probably the twelve thought Jesus would never get away if He once got mixed up with the children. Moreover, for various reasons they were now uneasy about attracting public attention. Before, they had welcomed publicity, while Jesus had constantly avoided it; now He is welcoming all challenges, and they are nervous and bewildered. Now His face is 'set like a flint' and they are following afar off. Luke 9⁵¹ makes it plain that the journey to Jerusalem has now begun; Jesus has once again warned His disciples of what is bound to happen there, and there is a new sternness noticeable in His words and on His face. But a new period demands a new chapter.

VIII. THE JOURNEY TO JERUSALEM

Before we set off for Jerusalem, we ought to notice that the teaching of Jesus has taken on a sharper edge. Satan, having failed with Jesus, is now at work amongst His disciples. Jesus had already told them that at the consummation of the age the Father would send His angels and gather 'all things that cause stumbling and cast them into the furnace of fire' (Mt. 13⁴¹⁻⁴²). Perhaps we have not given due weight to these warnings. There is a destructive fire, Jesus tells us, which burns up all waste products; and when a man has lost his soul, he becomes a 'waste product', that could turn Heaven itself into Hell. As Bunyan told us, there is a way to Hell from the very gate of Heaven.

In Mark 10¹ we learn that Jesus has come to the borders of Judaea and Perea, again accompanied by large crowds. Among them is the man whom we call the rich young ruler, whom Jesus is said to have 'loved'. The story of His dialogue with him is too familiar to need repeating here, but the amazement of His disciples at the fact that so likely a candidate was turned down is impressive. As the young man turns away Jesus says, 'Children, how hard it is to get into the Kingdom of God! It is easier for a camel to get through the eye of a needle than for a rich man to get into the Kingdom.' Many attempts have been made to soften the hard edge of this saying, one suggesting that little side-gates into Eastern cities are sometimes called 'needles-eyes'; but this is not really helpful. Quite deliberately Jesus is picturing the absurd, the impossible. 'Heavenly pilgrims travel light' is clearly implied.

The disciples retort, 'Who then can be saved?' If a rich man can't get to Heaven, who can? Jesus, looking searchingly at them, says, 'Humanly speaking it *is* impossible; but with God all things are possible.' Peter turns the subject by saying, 'We've already qualified by leaving all to follow you.' And Jesus answers, 'No one has left home for my sake and the gospel's, who will not get all back in this world—with persecutions—and in the world to come eternal life.' All the same, before the end comes, there will be a surprising number of changes in their order of pre-eminence. We know how true this is.

As they are now on the way to the capital, we can take a look at Jesus and His men. Those who followed Him—some left Him at this point, we are given to understand—were afraid. In greater detail He now tells them what is going to happen; and by 'the Son of Man' it is clear that He means no longer 'I' but 'we' (see Mt. 20^{18}). They did not understand, but they were afraid to ask Him. Two are not afraid, however; they have not forgotten the vision on Mount Hermon, when they saw Him in glory. According to Matthew they brought their mother Susanna to speak for them (Mt. 20^{20}). What they want is that they, James and John, should sit, one on His right and one on His left, in His glory. 'Can you share the Passion of which I have been telling you?' 'Yes,' they say. 'Some day you shall', He assures them. But there are no 'reserved seats'. We know that in the fullness of time the mother of the sons of Zebedee saw not her two sons, but two outcast criminals, one on the right hand of the King of Glory and one on the left (Mt. 27^{56}).

Meanwhile this rather selfish request arouses resentment among the twelve and Jesus tells them that the rule of the Kingdom is not ambition, but service; the 'favoured few' are to give their lives for the many. The phrase a 'ransom for many' has led to much controversy, but means what it says. The few have always thrown their lives away for the many and that is how the Church has grown throughout the ages. Surely 'the Son of Man' is a phrase which here concerns the behaviour not just of one individual but of a group?

There are many points of interest about the story of Bartimaeus. The first is his use of the title 'Son of David'. The second is the fact that Mark does not tell us who 'they' were, but we may guess that they were the disciples, who were anxious to get through Jericho without a scene. They were still nervous and uneasy, but Bartimaeus is not to be silenced. The third is an interesting variant reading of verse 50, 'He, *putting on* His garment' instead of 'throwing away His garment'; beggars will lie out in the sun with their cloaks by their sides in an Eastern street, but they will always gather their discarded garments about them when they rise to meet a superior.

Getting near Jerusalem, Jesus sends two of His disciples from the Mount of Olives to Bethany, which lies on the slope of Olivet facing Bethany. Bethany is clearly the 'village opposite to you'. The scene that follows is clearly prearranged. The demonstration that takes place on the Mount of Olives—not, it should be noticed, in the streets of the city—points to a great change in the mood of the disciples. It has been suggested that something must have taken place, to turn a nervous and embarrassed company into a triumphant multitude.

The raising of Lazarus might very well have been this factor in the situation. Nothing could have been better calculated to raise the drooping spirits of the company than such an outstanding miracle. The whole question of Lazarus rouses many problems that we cannot enter into here; the greatest being, of course, the total silence of the first three gospels. One suggestion has been that we have here a dramatic story of a man's conversion, told in the symbolic fashion of the fourth evangelist. Someone indeed 'dead'—'brought back to life'. According to the fourth gospel, the miracle was the turning point in the whole drama of Passion week, rousing the enemies of Jesus to desperation—'The whole world has gone after Him.'

Apart from this possible factor, the fact that other pilgrims must by now have joined them must have made a difference to the disciples' morale. They were no longer a small and bewildered company; a large and tumultuous crowd of Galileans had joined them and their spirits rose. This might seem to make our Lord's change of policy all the stranger. Why did He, who 'did not strive or cry, nor cause His voice to be heard in the streets' (Mt. 12$^{19, 20}$), now organize a demonstration which, if it was allowed to get out of hand, would be certain to bring Him into conflict with the authorities? Jerusalem would be full to overflowing at the Passover. Jew and Gentile came together: the forces of law and order, and angry crowds from Galilee, very ready for rebellion. Amid these explosive elements Jesus was already a suspected person.

It is evident that Jesus was determined to make a last and very open appeal to the Jewish people, once and for all to drop their desire for vengeance against Rome, which could only end in one way, and be content to fulfil God's purpose. In God's plan they should indeed win the gentile world, but by serving it; they should conquer, but by suffering. It was an entirely practical policy, and it might have changed the whole course of world history. If the Jews had been ready to make of their temple a 'house of prayer for all nations', the gentiles would have brought their wealth and glory into it. One has only to look at the map to see that Palestine is the natural bridge between East and West, North and South.

As the week went on, it was more and more obvious that Jesus' appeal would be made at the cost of His own life, and of how much more! He longed for a response from men; but in any case His appeal must be made and His Church would carry God's purpose through in the end. We are just beginning to do so now, but what a story it is! And how much suffering it has cost! Jews and Gentiles are gradually coming closer together and in face of the universal catastrophe which hovers over us all in these latter days, we are being *forced* together. He foresaw it all, and told us. First of all one Church, then one State; if not, destruction. And His verdict on man's obduracy and slowness to see has already been given; it is 'Father, forgive them, for they know not what they do', and then, 'Father, into Thy hand I commit My spirit.'

How far the tumultuous welcome which took place on Olivet pleased Jesus, we cannot tell. He dismounted from the ass and went unattended to the temple, where He 'looked round' on everything, as though taking stock of the situation. Some of the children were still shouting 'Hosanna' and the usual protests were made at the disturbance they were making. But Jesus defended them; the very stones would cry out, if they were silenced (Hab. 2[11]). He spent the night at Bethany.

Both Mark and John describe for us a feast at Bethany, though each of the evangelists tells the story of the anointing differently. Mark speaks of an unnamed woman making the gesture; John says it was Mary of Bethany. John says she poured the precious scent over His feet; Mark, over His head. John says it happened before the Triumphal entry; Mark, after it. Matthew follows Mark and Luke omits the story; though he has a story of another anointing, by a woman who was a sinner, at the house of Simon the Pharisee. Curiously enough, the host at the house in Bethany, according to Mark, is 'Simon the Leper'. All kinds of skin diseases were then called 'leprosy'. According to John, 'Lazarus' was at the supper table when Mary brought her gift. Out of this tangle of difficulties it is hard indeed to get a coherent story. We certainly cannot do without Luke's charming story (Lk. 7[36ff]); it is too lifelike for us to doubt is authenticity. But is not necessary to identify the woman who was a sinner with Mary Magdalene, though this has had great currency in Christian literature. This identification hangs on a slender thread indeed, the fact that the two characters appear fairly close together in Luke's Gospel— and on the similarities in the narratives. Nor is there any evidence that the 'seven demons' Jesus cast out had anything to do with prostitution. If the connection between these two women is broken, the further identification with Mary of Bethany becomes entirely gratuitous. Mary of Bethany may well have heard the Galilean story, and may have thought that she too would show her gratitude for Jesus having restored her brother to her, and in a similar way.

Another case of variant interpretations can be found in Mk 14[7 and 8], Jn 12[7]. Mark says the woman had come beforehand to anoint Jesus' body for burial. John, that Mary had been keeping the scent for His burial, but could not restrain herself and poured it out in love upon His living body. Perhaps, however, the best reading of John is, 'Let her keep it for the day of My burial', meaning that she will be glad to think, when the other women come to embalm His body, that she had showed her love to her Lord while He was still alive. If we agree that the woman was Mary, Mark 14[9] means that she must have a place wherever the Passion story is told.

A word must be said about Judas and his criticism of Mary's gift. John says that he was a thief, but the word 'thief' used here does not mean a robber in the modern sense of the word; it was a common term of abuse for any revolutionary. Barrabas was a 'robber', we read in John 19[40]; and similarly in saying 'All that ever came before me are thieves and robbers' (Jn 19[40]) Jesus was not charging all His predecessors with being thieves in the literal sense of the words, but with being revolutionaries.

IX. THE STORY OF HOLY WEEK

We have noticed that the story of the cleansing of the Temple comes at the beginning of the ministry in John, and at its close in the first three gospels. Of course, it may have happened twice, but it seems to have attracted little or no attention in John 2, and it surely fits better into the scheme of things at the beginning of the Passion Story than at the beginning of Christ's ministry. Even the fourth evangelist says, 'They [the disciples] remembered the words of Scripture, "zeal for Thy house will consume me"'; surely that is more appropriate to the Passion Story. Moreover, the reference that follows to the temple of His body (Jn 2[18, 19]) is out of place where it stands.

The wrath of Jesus was aroused not so much by the buyers and sellers in the Temple, but by the fact that the traffic was going on in the Court of the Gentiles. The Jews could keep their part of the Temple inviolate; in fact the 'middle wall of partition' kept the Gentiles out of it. Yet apparently anything could happen in the Court of the Gentiles. This was, as a matter of fact, a public thoroughfare, a short cut between two streets; and it had become a cattle-market. Jesus stopped the right of way (Mk 11[20]): 'My house shall be called a house of prayer for all nations,' He said. 'You have made it a den of thieves' (or perhaps butchers).

This action may also indicate Jesus' dislike of the sacrificial system; there is some evidence pointing this way. Matthew points out that He healed the blind and the lame in the Temple, and brought the children in 'to sing the place sweet' (Mt. 21[14, 15]). From Amos onwards there is a succession of prophetic protests against the sacrificial system (Amos 5[25], Hos. 6[6], Isa. 1[11], Jer. 7[22], Ps 40[6] and 50[7]). If Jesus was at this point making a public protest against the ceaseless slaughter of animals in the name of religion He would be in a great succession. For the moment there was no counter-demonstration; it was as if Christ's great gesture had been almost unnoticed, and ineffective. Was Jesus disappointed? Perhaps His thoughts at this time are reflected in the parable of the wicked husbandmen, in which He recognizes the facts of the situation.

Jesus' action has determined His enemies once and for all to dispose of Him. First of all, they ask Him by what authority He has acted in this way. He answers by putting His finger on the weak spot in their position—John the Baptist. Was he, or was he not, the greatest of the prophets? If they say he was, Jesus can reply, 'Why then, did you not accept his message, which included a vindication of My mission?' If they say he was not, they could be lynched, for John the Baptist was the hero of the hour. Their silence betrays their confusion, and Jesus goes on to tell them the naked truth.

Their next approach is more cautious; by bringing some of Herod's circle with them, they hope to entangle Him in some discussion which they can bring up before Pilate later, on the vexed question of the Roman taxes, which of course were bitterly resented. Jesus asks them to show Him a shilling. When it is produced, He turns the coin on one side, and says, 'Whose head is this?' They say, 'Why, Caesar's, of course.' Then He turns the coin the other way, and they answer, 'Some deity or other' (one of the gods of Rome). 'Very well,' says Jesus. 'Let Caesar have his share and the god have his!' This is one of the points where I have no doubt that some of my friends will differ from my interpretation; but I am convinced that any visit to a museum where Roman coins of the period are exhibited will endorse this reading. The real trouble about the orthodox interpretation is that the answer, printing a capital 'G' (to indicate God Himself) really settles nothing. It suggests that 'Caesar' and 'God' have separate dominions, which is surely rank heresy. In truth God rules over all. Jesus refused to commit Himself to the suggestion that He was against the taxes; obviously He was not.

The next question came from the Sadducees, and was intended to expose popular eschatology; it was a fantastic story invented for the purpose, but quite irrelevant. The answer Jesus gives contains a grave rebuke for their frivolity, and goes on to stress that sex relations as we know them will have no place in the future life. This does not of course mean that treasured ties will have no future meaning, but rather that they will be sublimated.

In the next discussion it is pleasant to find some agreement. It is not generally realized that there were some 'liberals' amongst Rabbinical theologians. There had been many attempts to summarize the law in one or two great principles. The Jews' formidable range of regulations—365 negative and 246 positive—could all be summed up in 'Thou shalt love the Lord Thy God . . . and thy neighbour as thyself.' This summary can be traced back to Hillel, who lived half a century before Jesus; but the negative form of 'the golden rule' not only preceded Jesus but survived Him. Here in Jerusalem Jesus found a kindred spirit. The last topic is introduced by Jesus Himself. He is not denying that Christ is the Son of David, but pointing out that there is a higher authority than David.

'The common people heard Him gladly', Mark notes at this point. They thoroughly appreciated His attacks on the Scribes, who have a chapter to themselves in Matthew 23. It is not my purpose to discuss this chapter, about which some of the most devoted followers of Jesus have often been uneasy. I have never heard it read in public. It is as if we were ourselves before the judgement seat; here is a list of the sins to which ministers and preachers of the Gospel are most prone. But it is fair to say that Jesus is not attacking the Pharisees as a party, but rather the less reputable scribes of the Pharisaic party. With that proviso, we as preachers do well to take heed; for these are sins of which we ourselves are more likely to be guilty than are our people. Neither is it my intention to expound Mark 13 in detail. This sombre forecast of the future is not in the same style as the rest of the gospel. Possibly it is a part or the whole of the eschatological flysheet which Eusebius says came to the Christians of Jerusalem just before the fall of the city. Notice the phrase 'Let the reader make a note of this', which implies a written document. It may have been added to this gospel after it was written.

The parable of the porter at the end of the chapter, and the prophecy of destruction of the Temple at the beginning, probably come from the original gospel. The first of these two passages is particularly important, because it motivates the rest of the drama. At some time Jesus did prophesy the destruction of the Temple, and the fall of the city—to some of His twelve at least—and it was this, I am convinced, that led to His betrayal and arrest by the Roman authorities. In Mark 14[58] we read, 'We heard this man say, I will destroy this temple, and raise up another not made with hands in three days.' Putting this beside John 2[19], we may say that this is a garbled version of something He had said; it was 'Destroy this temple and I will raise it up in three days'; the fourth evangelist explains that Jesus was speaking of His body.

From the Wednesday onwards of this fateful week events moved quickly. The arrangements for the Last Supper were evidently made beforehand. Mark says that the two disciples were to follow a *man* carrying a waterpot (a very rare sight in an Eastern city). Matthew tells us that they went to the house of Mr X. The host of the Upper Room has sometimes been identified with 'the disciple whom Jesus loved' and he again with the rich young ruler and even with Lazarus whom, we read, 'Jesus loved'. It is unlikely that this supper was the actual passover-meal, for that was not partaken of until the Friday night; John 18[28] says that the priests had not eaten their passover on Good Friday morning. Perhaps it was the Qiddush, a meal taken on Thursday evening to welcome the coming of the great day of the feast. This was a meal at which bread and wine were taken, and prayers read, which began at 6 p.m. on the Thursday and culminated with the passover-supper on Friday evening.

The first thing that happened when the disciples met was that Jesus washed their feet, including those of Judas. Peter protested, but Jesus told him that he would understand what this meant later on. It is significant that Jesus was now talking about 'later on'; so far it had been 'now'. 'Now is the judgment of this world; now shall the prince of this world be cast out, and I, if I be lifted up, shall draw all men to Myself.' Now His mood seemed to have changed, and He talks of 'later on': 'Whither I go, you cannot follow Me now, but you shall follow Me afterwards.' This must have been exceedingly perplexing to the twelve. They had come to the supper-table all tense about an imminent crisis; and now it would seem they were being put off with talk of later events. 'Why cannot I follow Thee now?' Peter asked. Jesus answered by telling Peter that, if He did not wash him, He could do nothing for him; so the swift reply comes, 'Lord, not my feet only then, but also my hands and my head!' Peter was always humble; that was why he was first. John 13[10] may be an allusion—and the last discourses of Jesus are full of such—to the wedding service. The passover ritual was modelled on the idea of the 'marriage' of God's people to their bridegroom. In Judaism the bride's feet were washed, not because they were soiled, but to remove any dust still clinging to them from her father's house. From henceforth she must belong to her husband. Just as, in an English wedding, the father 'gives the bride away' to her husband, so the washing of the bride's feet in an Eastern and also in a Roman wedding symbolized the fact that she had changed her family. So Jesus may be explaining to Peter that He is not now so much cleansing him, but rather uniting him to Himself for ever.

In the sacrament which follows, though it is (strangely) omitted by the fourth gospel, the bread symbolizes the life given for the life of the world (Jn 6[33]), and the cup the blood shed for the life of the Church (Acts 20[28]); it is the blood of the covenant, between God and His people. Jesus is saying farewell to His disciples until the day when He drinks the new wine with them in the Kingdom of God. After the singing of a psalm they went out to the Mount of Olives.

The last discourses, so familiar and so dear, are at every turn reminiscent of the passover ritual. The most encouraging thing about them is the fact that, though Jesus' mind is shadowed by dark fears for His own people and for the world, He has no fears for the Church. If only we will love one another, and keep in our memory His words, which have such cleansing and enabling power, He has no fears for us. His words will cleanse our souls, and keep us true. Even what we cannot understand will be kept ever before us. The day will never come when we can say, 'Now we can do without Him; we have learned enough' but the Holy Spirit (His *alter ego*) shall guide us into all truth. The Spirit will 'convict the world of sin'. All we have to do is to keep His words in our minds and obey them. This is very inadequate as an exposition of what is to many readers the most precious part of the Bible. I feel that, to do anything like justice to these chapters, I should need to write on nothing else!

So they leave the upper room and come to Gethsemane. Now all but Peter, James, and John are left behind. They alone hear Jesus agonize in prayer. We can tell something of the depth of sorrow in that dark hour by the fact that He uses the word 'if'; 'If it be possible let this cup pass from Me' (Mt. 26[39]). He who always protested against the word 'if' is using it Himself. All the tragedy of history was passing through His soul; Judas, the Jewish people, the whole story of human destiny. Three times He repeats the same prayer, and three times He comes and finds them sleeping—'for sorrow', Luke says.

And now Jesus is betrayed, delivered up, by Judas. Why did they never suspect Judas? When he went out from the supper-table, they thought he was going out to buy something that was lacking for the feast. Judas had answered with the rest, 'Surely it can't be I?' And Jesus had answered, 'Surely not.' If the disciples had known where Judas was really going, there would have been an attempt to stop him by force. Jesus had done everything to warn Judas of his danger, and had tried to save him from himself. Now He greets him with the old title: 'Comrade, what are you doing here?' Here He is quoting the actual words probably engraved on the cup from which He and Judas had been drinking the same evening. 'Comrade, what are you here for? Have a good time while you can.' That inscription has been discovered engraved on several drinking cups and vessels of this period. The attempt of Peter to rescue his Master was at any rate a valiant effort. Only the fourth evangelist tells us it was Peter, but we might have guessed it; though Peter himself says nothing about it—in Mark 14[47] he is simply described as 'one of those standing about'.

By this time James and John have disappeared in the darkness, and Peter is left alone with 'another disciple' who, says the fourth evangelist, was 'well-known to the high-priest, and had the entry to the high-priest's establishment'. So it was that Peter got into the courtyard of Caiaphas' house. Annas was really the head of the high-priestly family; he had been deposed by the Romans, but had managed by bribery to get his relatives appointed in his place; and his son-in-law Caiaphas was in office that year. Yet Annas remained at the centre of things. So Jesus faced them both when He was brought to Caiaphas' house. There His enemies were unable to get satisfactory evidence that He had in fact threatened to destroy the Temple. The evidence of one man was not sufficient, so they asked Him directly to say on His oath whether He was the Son of God.

The evangelists report Jesus' answer in different forms. Mark has 'I am'; Matthew, 'Thou hast said'; and Luke 'You say that I am.' A large number of texts question the 'I am' of Mark, and have 'Thou hast said that I am', with Luke. I think we must say that it is doubtful whether Jesus did say 'I am' in so many words, in answer to the question. 'Thou sayest' or 'Thou hast said' means, according to some scholars, not 'Yes' but 'That is how you put it' or 'The words are yours'. 'Henceforth,' Jesus says, 'you shall see the Son of Man sitting on the right hand of God and coming with the clouds of Heaven.' This the high-priest professed to regard as blasphemy, and tore his robe as a protest.

We come back to Peter, warming himself outside at the fire in the courtyard. It is pathetic to see the fisherman the butt of servant-girls and others. Perhaps he would have made a better show of it if he had not been identified right away as the man who was with Jesus in the garden, the same man who recklessly fought for Him, and who had been snubbed for his pains. Perhaps he thought, I must not implicate my Master in that futile resistance. And on the spur of the moment he said, 'I'm not the man you mean; I don't know what you're talking about', and with that first lie he got caught in a web, and all his cursing and swearing could not get him out of it, or save him from humiliation. He was like a beast in a net struggling to break out. At last he did get away, and went out shaking with sobs. He had given himself away with every word. By yet another chain he was bound to Jesus.

I suppose it did not dawn upon Peter then that, if he had been dealing not just with the servants but with the masters instead he might have been crucified himself; for it was a criminal offence to draw a sword and use it at that time of the passover. However, 'the disciple whom Jesus loved' befriended him and took him away. Before Peter left the courtyard he caught a glimpse, says Luke, of His Master, who was bound and waiting to be taken before Pilate. Their eyes met. It was a moment Peter was never to forget.

In the early morning Jesus was taken before Pilate. Here we have another variation between the fourth gospel and the synoptics. The fourth evangelist says it was first thing in the morning; but according to Mark there was first a meeting of the Sanhedrin. We have no means of knowing how long this meeting lasted. Its members must have been in a chastened and sober mood after the disgraceful scenes of the night before, in which all sorts of insults had been heaped upon the prisoner; it was necessary to restore the dignity of the Sanhedrin before appearing in public. Apparently it was not a regular or strictly constitutional meeting; probably it was hastily summoned and with such people as Nicodemus and Joseph of Arimathea (who were known to be sympathetic towards the prisoner) excluded. There they took a vote, by acclamation, condemning Jesus; and so He was brought to Pilate. It is evident that great efforts were made behind the scenes to influence Pilate; Jesus Himself says, in answer to Pilate's first question, 'Are you saying this of yourself, or have others been talking about Me?' (Jn 18[34]). Again, it will be noticed that Jesus says, not 'I am a king', but 'You say that I am a king' (verse 37).

Pilate was impressed, in spite of himself. His wife, who was related to the imperial family, and who was already interested in Judaism, was more impressed still. But it was really a foregone conclusion; the Sanhedrin's vote had really prejudged and settled the issue. Pilate could not afford another riot; he had burnt his fingers badly already, and knew that he would be recalled to Rome in disgrace if there was any trouble this time at the passover. So it is quite clear that when the priests shouted, 'If thou lettest this man go, thou art not Caesar's friend', they were playing their trump card; Pilate, who was a coward, gave way. The crown of thorns and the sceptre were crude jests by the soldiers, more a matter of Jew-baiting than of personal hatred for the prisoner.

The rest of the story, the choice of Barabbas by the crowd, and the unavailing attempt of Pilate's wife to save Jesus, are too familiar to need repetition; but one or two points deepen and sharpen our sense of tragedy. Apparently Barabbas was also called 'Jesus', a very common Jewish name in those days; in the oldest version of Matthew and John we read of Jesus Barabbas (Mt.

27^{16}, Jn 19^{40}). It is doubtful whether it really was the custom to release one prisoner at the passover; this was evidently an offer made to conciliate the mob. Pilate probably expected that they would shout for Jesus, when it came to the point; for he knew how popular Jesus had been only a week or so before. In a sense his wife Claudia had by her intervention turned the scale against Jesus. The scribes were clever enough not to take direct action themselves, but their agents passed round the word that Barabbas was the man to ask for; when Pilate faced the crowd again, the issue was settled, and Pilate knew that he would have to give way. The fact was that most of the demonstrators hated Pilate more than they loved Jesus, and in a sense His fate was sealed when they realized that Pilate was on His side.

We have to understand their point of view. A passionately race-conscious people had seen in Jesus a potential leader. He had raised their hopes—though they misunderstood His words—and then seemingly had failed them utterly. When they had hailed Him as 'King of the Jews', they had expected Him to lead them against the power of Rome; now He had let Himself be arrested without a blow. Barabbas at least had fought bravely and suffered for the people's cause. They had forgotten all about him lately, but the comparison was marked; and now loyalty to a lost leader had something to do with their cries.

It was still quite early in the morning. By nine o'clock Jesus had been raised upon the Cross. The gospels all tell us of the setting up of the crosses, but they do not dwell on the agony. (The same thing is true of the scourging before Pilate; we can imagine how a modern writer would have let himself go about the cruelty of it all.) Their restraint is almost miraculous. In the fourth gospel every trace of suffering and shame is gone. The only suggestion comes in the simple words 'I thirst'. For the fourth evangelist the Passion has become the 'glory' of Jesus; and even in the other gospels there is a lessening of tension when we leave Pilate's hall. We are told that Jesus refused the drug that was offered Him. There was His mother to see to; somebody must take care of her in Jerusalem, and the disciple whom He loved was standing by, ready to take her away from it all. There were the crowds of people still about Him as they had always been, and He prays, 'Father, forgive them; they don't know what they are doing.'

But what about that very different word from the Cross, 'the cry of dereliction'? Many explanations of this cry have been offered, but none can explain it away. It does not become less impressive. We may believe that here at last our Lord became fully one with His people, that for one moment the tragedy of Jewish history and of world history overwhelmed His spirit, coming between Himself and the Father and momentarily blotting out that light which was His life. In that moment the world was redeemed. 'It is finished' was His next word, and 'Father, into Thy hands I commend My Spirit' the last.

Every word in this part of the Gospel story is full of meaning. 'His blood be upon us and upon our children' was the reckless cry of a maddened crowd; but it became one of the greatest of Christian prayers ('His blood be upon us and ever abide'). So it is all through. The fourth evangelist says, 'He gave up His spirit.' He had said, 'The Son of Man hath not where to lay His head'; now at last His head drops to rest on the Cross. The Vatican text of Matthew tells us that a soldier pierced His side before death, and 'set His spirit free'. Men had sought to bind Him with the bonds of death; yet now paradoxically His redeeming Spirit is set free, free to possess the lives of His disciples, to empower them and to impel them to go on, and to go out, until they cover the world with His fame. So far He has had to struggle almost alone to play the part of the Son of Man; now His Spirit possesses His disciples—and can possess us too, if we have learned the lesson of the Cross. Again John, speaking of the spear-thrust, tells us also of the water and the blood; and in his first epistle he writes 'This is He that came by water and blood—not with the water only, but with the water and the blood—and it is the Spirit that bears witness. 'For there are three who bear witness: the Spirit, and the water, and the blood' (1 Jn 5$^{6-8}$).

What this passage means is that there is a close connexion between the death of Jesus and the gift of the Spirit, and this binds the whole gospel together. So it is that the fourth gospel tells us that after that first Easter Jesus breathed upon His disciples and said, 'Receive ye the Holy Ghost' (Jn 20^{22}) and He showed them His hands and His side. The Passion and the gift go together.

I have left myself no space to dwell upon the Easter story and its tremendous significance, though the record is incomplete without it. The riddle of the Resurrection appearances should be studied with the help of a book like *The Risen Master* (Latham); a book which is old yet still far from out of date. And as you study and ponder, pray that you may never lose your sense of wonder.

3. The Letter to the Colossians

By the Rev. John H. Chamberlayne, M.A., M.Th., Ph.D.

INTRODUCTION

This letter is a very interesting one, giving us some of Paul's greatest thoughts, but it is not altogether an easy one. Therefore it helps to know a little about the background of the place, and the writer's connection with it and with the Church there.

The city of Colosse lay close to other important cities, namely, Laodicea and Hierapolis, in the Roman province of Asia. The city lay on both sides of the River Lycus, about one hundred miles from Ephesus. This river valley was subject to earthquakes and was very beautiful, with wealthy industries in cloth-making and dyeing. Although formerly a town of some position, yet by the time that Paul addressed his letter there it had become a place of smaller influence. Nevertheless, even though, as J. B. Lightfoot wrote, Colosse was the most unimportant town to which Paul ever wrote a letter, it was here that there arose a dangerous heresy which threatened to cause trouble to the faith of believers. Therefore he wrote to set clearly before them the wonder and the all-sufficiency of the Lord in whom they believed.

To this area there had come many Jewish families. Some had been transported there by Antiochus the Great many years before, but others had no doubt come as traders to share in the prosperity of the cities in this valley. It was possibly to the Jewish settlements there that Christian missionaries first came to proclaim 'the glad tidings of salvation'. We are informed that during Paul's three years' stay in Ephesus the whole province of Asia was evangelized, so that all those in the province, both Jews and Greeks, heard the word of the Lord (Acts 19[10]). Probably during this time the preachers came to Colosse.

We do not know the name of the actual founder or founders of the Church there. It is clear that Paul did not do so, nor had he visited it. He writes that they, like the Laodiceans, had not seen his face in the flesh (2[1]), yet it is probable that his preaching and inspiration had directed those who first planted the Church in Colosse. (Though we may not visit a town, our preaching can take the seed to others, and bear fruit in new churches in new

140

places.) The minister of the Church there appears to have been Epaphras, whom Paul also describes as his fellow-servant (1^7) and who is connected with the Churches in Laodicea and Hierapolis ($4^{12, 13}$). Epaphras may have been the founder-pastor of the Church in Colosse.

Although there were many Jews in this area, it seems that the Church there was mainly a Gentile one. He refers to them as 'being in time past alienated and enemies in your mind' (1^{21})—a phrase similar to one used in Ephesians to describe those who are 'strangers from the covenants of the promise' (Eph. $2^{1-2 \text{ and } 12}$). Paul also refers here to God's goodness in 'the glory of the mystery of Christ among the Gentiles, which is Christ in you' (Colos. 1^{27}), and in this he appears to be speaking to their condition. Furthermore, the list of sins (mentioned in 3^{5-7}) are more particularly Gentile ones, from which we may infer that this was mainly a Gentile Christian community. As we are Gentiles, Paul writes for us.

From this Church, there came news of strange doctrines which threatened to make havoc of the faith of some believers. It may well have been that Epaphras bore the news. It was not all bad news. Paul gives thanks for their faith in Christ and for their love of the saints (1^4), for the increasing fruit among them and for their love in the Spirit, of which Epaphras has told him ($1^{6 \text{ and } 7}$). His prayer that these gifts may increase is a fine example of pastoral care for these disciples, to whom his heart goes out ($1^{9, 10\text{ff}}$). But the news of the strange doctrines rouses his concern as a teacher of the faith, to warn them lest they are led away and to equip them with new knowledge to meet the arguments of opponents.

We cannot be sure about the nature of 'The Colossian Heresy', which has been a subject of much controversy among New Testament scholars. The description of the heresy in the letter is fragmentary, and attempts to identify it with later more developed heretical movements have not been satisfactory. It appears rather that Paul is warning the converts against certain *tendencies* in belief, which at a later time became more apparent in fully fledged heretical movements. There are in this letter certain ideas which Paul goes to great trouble to emphasize because he believes that there are those who have wrong conceptions of the faith, conceptions which might cause ruin to the Church.

He emphasizes the unique supremacy of Christ, 'the image of the invisible God; in Him all fulness dwells' ($1^{15, 19}$). In Him are hid all the treasures of wisdom and knowledge (2^2) and in Him dwells the fulness of the Godhead in bodily form (2^9). This high view of the Christ is to combat those views which would place Christ on a lower plane. It has been claimed that this view of Christ is far in advance of Paul's position at the time, and that it belongs to a later period. On the other hand the situation at Colosse, and the threat to the Church, may well have called forth from Paul his loftiest conceptions, of which we have clues in other letters. He has been forced to think out the implications of his own faith by the very pressure of events—an exercise to which we are all driven from time to time.

This supremacy of Christ is revealed in His part in the work of creation; by Him were all things created (1^{16}). In Him all things hold together (1^{17}). Yet this same Lord was flesh and blood, who in the body of His flesh did His work of redemption (1^{22}) and who in His bodily form revealed the fulness of the Godhead. The exaltation of Christ is not allowed to displace the reality of His humanity.

Other factors in these heretical tendencies at Colosse will become clear in the course of the commentary. They include astrological elements (horoscopes are still with us!), here referred to as 'the rudiments of the world' (2^8), i.e. the 'stoicheia' or elemental spirits of the world, spirits of the stars and planets. There were also demonic powers, to which reference is made as 'principalities and powers' (1^{16}, 2^{10} and 2^{15}). It was a demon-haunted universe. There were philosophical elements (2^8) and a ritualistic emphasis on festivals, new moons and sabbaths (2^{16}), together with ascetic elements, and the laying down of laws concerning food and drink (2^{16}). In the midst of a morally lax society, there was a danger of licence in the Church—a lack of control over sex relations and passions (3^{5-8})—whilst angel worship also formed a part of the same group of beliefs (2^{18}).

At a later time, the beliefs which are seen in embryo in this letter took a more definite form in the various systems which come under the term Gnosticism, the cult which held that matter itself is essentially evil and also eternal. It was believed that by secret lore and philosophical speculations man might through many stages reach God. Paul stresses that he longs to 'present *every man* perfect in Jesus Christ', that is, Christ is for the slow and foolish as well as the cultured and clever (3^{11}).

Some scholars have questioned the genuineness of this epistle, its Pauline authorship. One objection has been the lack of external evidence, which is rather slight in the period A.D. 100–160. Again there is a marked peculiarity in the choice of words and in the slow, rather laboured style. The Gnostic teaching contended with here has been claimed by some to belong to a later date. The view of the nature of Christ is more advanced than in most of Paul's other letters and there is an absence of characteristic Pauline ideas, e.g. Justification by Faith, Adoption, and the work of the Spirit. At one time the unity of the letter was also questioned.

However, these objections may be met by the study of the epistle. In the early years of the 1st century, *Ephesians* was a popular letter and overshadowed *Colossians*, on which account the latter figures less in early Christian literature. The peculiarity of the terms which Paul uses, and the style, are in part dictated by the subject he is discussing, so that he uses the terms of his opponents in discussing these topics. The objection to the letter on the ground of its references to Gnostic teaching has been considered above, whilst the developed Christology is seen to be a reflection of teaching found also elsewhere in Paul's letters (I Cor. 8[6]; Rom. 11[36]; I Cor. 2[6]; II Cor. 4[4]). The lack of sound characteristic Pauline terms may well be due to the difference in circumstances as compared with his letters to the Galatians and the Romans.

This letter appears to be closely connected with *Ephesians* and *Philemon*. It is generally accepted that all three were written in Rome, during the period of Paul's imprisonment (A.D. 62–64), although some scholars have sought to date them earlier, during Paul's Caesarean imprisonment (A.D. 60–62), referred to in Acts 24[26-27]. The developed character of the letter's theology makes the latter suggestion less likely. Others again have suggested that Paul wrote these letters from an imprisonment in Ephesus at a still earlier date (A.D. 53–55), which would seem even less likely. In any case, from his prison Paul sent these letters by the hands of Tychicus and Onesimus (4[7-9]). There is also reference to a letter from Laodicea (4[16]), which has to be considered later.

It is most helpful to use a good standard commentary in the study of this epistle. The volume in the *Moffatt Commentary* series on these three imprisonment writings is by E. F. Scott, who is a very fine and clear expositor. In the *Cambridge New Testament* series, there is a volume by C. F. D. Moule which is very useful. C. H. Dodd's *Meaning of Paul for Today* throws light on the mind of Paul, whilst *A Theological Word Book of the Bibles* (S.C.M.), edited by Alan Richardson, will prove invaluable in clarifying the use of the words Paul uses. Take note also of the renderings that different Bible translations gives to a passage, by using the *Revised Standard Version* (*RSV*), the *New English Bible* (*NEB*), and others, alongside your *Revised Version*. But it is helpful to have one version, possibly the *Revised Version*, for regular use, from which important passages can be committed to memory. Then you will be able to quote correctly and with ease, as well as finding verses without delay. To your study bring in all possible references from elsewhere that may help to a fuller understanding of this epistle.

It is our hope that this commentary may serve as a tool, to help you as you gather material about this letter. An interleaved Bible is useful in which to make your own notes. Remember above all, as you study, that you will receive the help of the Holy Spirit in this work, to equip you to become a more effective preacher of the Gospel.

A. *CHRISTIAN SUCCESS*
(Col. 1$^{1-14}$)

The letter opens with a simple word of greeting. It comes from Paul, 'an apostle of Christ Jesus through the will of God' and from Timothy 'our brother'. It is sent to 'the saints and faithful brethren in Christ at Colosse'. Then we find the greeting, which is used to open all the Pauline letters: 'Grace to you and peace from God our Father.'

Paul writes as an 'apostle' (literally, 'one who is sent forth'). In his letters, he practically always means 'an apostle of Christ' in using this term, because he insists that he is 'an apostle, not from man or through man, but through Jesus Christ and God the Father' (Gal. 1^1). It is moreover clear that the term 'apostle' was not confined to the original Twelve whom Jesus chose (Lk. 6^{13}) but was used more widely. Thus the Risen Lord appeared 'to the twelve . . . then to all the apostles' (I Cor. 15$^{5, 7}$; cp. Rom. 16^7). John Wesley had a similar conviction that he had been sent forth by God to a world parish. The word of Jesus, 'I have chosen you' (Jn 15^{16}) needs to be the conviction of every true Christian preacher.

Timothy is 'our brother', a title which is also given to others (Sosthenes (I Cor. 1^1) and Apollos (I Cor. 16^{12})). This young man was privileged to serve with Paul, yet how costly is this call, 'Put me to what Thou wilt, rank me with whom Thou wilt'; yet this is the hall-mark of brotherhood in Christ.

The Church members are addressed as 'the saints' and 'faithful brethren'. The term 'saints' has had a number of strange associations in the course of its history, but in its origin the term came from a cult concept meaning 'separate', 'set apart' for the use of a deity. At an early date, it was used in regard to things, such as 'holy garments', 'holy shewbread' and 'holy sacrifice'. In the New Testament, it is used of Christians as persons who are 'set apart for God's purposes' (cf. 'Saint': *Theological Word Book of the Bible*). These Christians are also described as 'faithful brethren in Christ . . . at Colosse'. They are living in two spheres, 'in Christ' and 'at Colosse'. It is part of the Apostle's task to help them to live in *both* spheres, in accord with the will of God. As the Christian lives in Christ as 'his native air', so such fellowship fills the more local sphere of life as well.

1³⁻⁸. As a wise teacher, Paul's first word is one of encouragement and assurance. The faith of these people and their love for the Church evokes a note of thankfulness, however much he may later need to admonish them for their weaknesses. Paul begins, not as a grumbler or censor but as a thankful guide, wanting to strengthen them.

Faith, hope, and love were, for Paul, the three abiding gifts (I Cor. 13¹³) and they are found together here. Faith and love depend on the hope laid up in heaven. What is this hope? As C. F. D. Moule has described it, this hope is the certainty that in spite of the world's ways and the world's standards God's way of love has the last word. In Donald Hankey's phrase, it is 'betting your life that there is a God', with the dependence on His love which is rooted in that certainty.

These gifts have come 'in the word of the truth of the gospel'. This gospel message has many facets. It is the truth, it is universal ('in all the world') and it is fruit-bearing. An increase among the hearers was to be expected, as the grace of God is active through the message. But this is only possible as the messengers are faithful. For the Colossians, Paul recalls that his fellow-servant and their faithful minister is Epaphras, who constantly 'strives in his prayers for them' (4¹²). The Lord's dependence on His human witnesses cannot be replaced by automation or by the record player. His world has to become incarnate again in us, who are called to pass it on to others.

1⁹⁻¹¹. Therefore, Paul describes the content of his prayer for them. It appears that his thought for them has progressive stages. He prays (i) that they may be filled with the knowledge of God's will. Then there will follow (ii) fitting conduct ('walk worthily of the Lord'). This is made possible by (iii) God's enabling power. Each of these three stages is qualified by phrases which are of interest. The knowledge of God's will grows by a deepening of spiritual wisdom and practical understanding. The man of right conduct will be 'in favour with God and man' (Lk. 2^{52}), with good works of every kind, bringing yet more knowledge of God. Such conduct will be sustained by the power of God, by patience to win through, by longsuffering with people and by an unquenchable joy (verse 11).

1$^{12-14}$. Paul's note of thanksgiving breaks through, whether he is in prison or out! Now he bids the Church be thankful, in the knowledge that the Father has made the Gentiles heirs of the kingdom. His readers were previously outside the covenants of promise, but God in His mercy has drawn back the veil to reveal His age-long purpose—that the Gentiles and the Jews ('us') should be heirs together of the kingdom (cp. Eph. 1$^{9-11}$).

Note the series of pictures used to describe God's action. God has given us a share in the 'realm of light' by rescuing us from darkness, and granting us freedom and forgiveness by the triumph which Christ won. The term which Paul uses for 'translated us' (*NEB* 'Brought us away') was used for the ancient practice of transferring whole populations from one country to another, after a greater power had conquered a smaller nation. Thus Israel and Judah were carried away into captivity into strange lands at an earlier period. Christ the conqueror has triumphed and has carried those under His sway into a new realm, in which there is freedom from former slavery, and forgiveness for those who have rebelled against the Father's will.

B. *THE SUFFICIENCY OF CHRIST*
(Col. 1$^{15-23}$)

The triumph of Christ is now described in glowing terms, as Paul tells these Christian converts the true nature of the Conqueror. This 'dear Son' is no ordinary human leader but has a far greater significance. As opposed to those thinkers (known as Gnostics)—who regarded the material world as evil, and created by a lesser divine being than the true God, and who regarded Jesus Christ as on a lower plane and status than God—Paul clearly asserts that Christ is 'the image of the invisible God' and the agent of God in all things in creation. The Apostle has no limit to the terms he uses to express the supremacy of Christ.

This supremacy is seen first in creation. Christ is described as God's 'image' (Gk. 'eikon'), which may mean either the 'likeness' or the manifestation of God (cp. II Cor. 4⁴). This high claim could be given only to Christ—He is God manifested. Therefore, He is before all created things. Whereas false teachers sought to regard Christ as a lesser being, one among other created beings, Paul claims that 'in Christ' everything has in fact been created.

Not content with so tremendous a claim, Paul also says that the whole created universe was created 'for Him'. This may well mean that such was the Father's love for the Son that He created a world to express that love in creative action. Everything is within that gift of creation which the Father undertook for the sake of the Son. It includes things in heaven and on earth, invisible and visible, thrones, sovereignties, powers and authorities of all kinds—'the whole universe has been created through him and for him' (*NEB*). On this account, far from being a created being, Christ existed before everything else and all things 'hold together' in Him. As the spokes of a wheel are able to move the cart because they are joined at the hub of the wheel, so the universe depends upon Christ as the hub of its life. He is the beginning of creation, the goal of creation and the power that holds creation together.

Few passages described so succinctly the relationship of Christ to the cosmic activities which serve as the environment for the life of man. As Paul sees it, nothing is beyond the control of Christ, because everything has been called into being through His activity and for love of Him.

Moreover, one part of the created order has a special relationship to Him. This part is that Body of which He is the Head, namely the Church. As He began everything else, so He is the origin of the Church (cp. Heb. 12¹). Always in Paul's mind the origin of the Church is linked with the fact of the Resurrection of Christ; so here we find that Christ is the Author of the Church because He was the first to return from the dead. This gave Him supremacy over all realms, whether of the living or the dead.

The crescendo of acclaim for Christ reaches its peak as Paul continues, that 'in him the complete being of God, by God's own choice, came to dwell' (*NEB*: verse 19). Every other claim pales into insignificance before this supreme act of the Father's grace and love.

What was the intention of God in the work of Christ? What purpose lay behind the coming of Christ to men? This may be summed up in two great words—Reconciliation and Holiness.

Reconciliation has a prominent place in the thought of Paul. Apart from I Corinthians 7^{11} (which refers to a wife's reconciliation to her husband), he uses on twelve occasions either the noun or the two verbs which express the idea of the changed relations between God and man, which has been effected by the death and resurrection of Christ. The initiative is seen as God's, and its object is the world of men, which has been apart from Him. Noteworthy among these uses are the verses in Romans 5^{10-11} and in II Corinthians 5^{18-20}. The hostility which lay between man in his need and sin and God in His 'separateness' and Justice has been overcome by the grace of God revealed in Christ.

As Paul has been dealing with the cosmic and universal significance of Christ's being, so the work of reconciliation is deemed in this passage to have a similar corporate and cosmic scope. Through the death of Christ all things (earthly as well as heavenly) are to be reconciled to God. This has a personal significance also; Paul reminds his readers in another letter that Jew and Gentile have been brought together into the household of God by Christ's work (Eph. 2^{16}).

Linked in these passages are the act of reconciliation and the death of Christ. The fact of estrangement in men's relationships is revealed in the sinful act of the Cross. Men's evil works led to such a result. But alienation and evil works did not have the last word as far as God's love was concerned. God did not spare His own Son but delivered Him up for us all (Rom. 8^{32}) and Paul continues, 'how shall He not with Him also give us all things?' Nothing was too much for God's love.

This reconciliation is the work of Christ's humanity, as Paul stresses: 'in the body of his flesh through death' (verse 22). It is no ethereal spirit or heavenly being but the human Jesus Christ through whom and in whom God acted. He has come to reconcile 'all things' to God, which recalls Paul's famous sentence, when he wrote that 'the created universe waits with eager expectation for God's sons to be revealed' (Rom. 8^{19}, *NEB*). All creation is involved in the work of Christ.

But what is the fruit of reconciliation? The great sacrificial work of Calvary must have a goal, a fulfilment. And this is, that those who have been separated from God should share His nature of holiness and purity. As Irenaeus wrote, about the year 185, for every Christian preacher to have a clear idea of the aim of each sermon, as well as a more ultimate purpose in his preaching as a whole.

1^{24}. Paul sought to identify his life and work with that of his Lord (as Gal. 2^{20} shows). Here the Apostle makes the bold claim that his sufferings for the faith, of which we catch a glimpse in II Corinthians 11^{23-28}, are a fulfilment of the sufferings of Christ. He is imprisoned on behalf of the Church, that is, for the sake of his readers. But, for him, these tribulations have a far wider significance. (a) It is a joy for him to have to undergo trials for his Lord and the Church. This is characteristic of the early Christian leaders who, like Peter and John, rejoiced 'that they were counted worthy to suffer dishonour for the Name' (Acts 5^{41}). So too Paul wrote to the Church in Corinth, 'I overflow with joy in all our affliction' (II Cor. 7^4). In the light of the variety and number of his tribulations, the continual note of joy is no surface effervescence but rises from an inner spring (cp. Jn 7^{38}, *NEB*). This overflowing joy is a hall-mark of the saints. When Brother Lawrence sought to practise the Presence of God, we find among his 'Maxims' that this practice is 'the schooling of the soul to find its joy in His Divine Companionship'. It is a joy that comes through suffering. (b) This suffering is not merely asceticism for the sake of keeping the body under control, though that has its value (I Cor. 9^{27}). It is a sharing in the redemptive work of Christ, so that the work of the Cross may come to its full fruition. This is no 'primrose path' to easy victory but a path of a hero seeking eternal glory. As Thomas à Kempis wrote, 'Jesus hath many who desire consolations and few desiring tribulations' and continues, 'All desire to joy with him; but few will suffer any pain for him' (chap. 11). Paul brings the two thoughts together—joy and pain —which are shared with Christ in His afflictions.

The work of Christ, in one sense, was completed on the Cross, as we see from Colossians 2^{14-15}. He has won an open triumph over evil powers. But the 'mopping-up' operations which follow from that central victory remain for the Church, which is the Body of Christ. 'Pockets of evil' continue to resist and can only be overcome at the cost of suffering. As we who are the Church seek to overcome these forces of evil, so we 'fill up that which is lacking of the afflictions of Christ'. (c) 'For his body's sake.' In his first letter to Corinth, Paul made use of this simile of the body (as representing a community: chap 12^{12-27}). This idea of the body is used by the Roman historian, Livy, and by Stoic writers of the

'He was made as we are in order that we might be made as |
Paul describes this aim in simple terms: 'to present you
and without blemish and unreproveable before him' (vers
The first part of this phrase we find in Ephesians 1^4, whil
term 'unreproveable' is also found in I Corinthians 1^8.
quality of life is stressed in similar terms in the words: 'th
may present every man perfect in Christ' (verse 28). 'Pe
(*teleios*) is used in the Septuagint (the Greek version of the
Testament) to mean that a sacrificial offering is sound, whole
without blemish. The spiritual and moral progress of his
verts has this goal for Paul. He will be satisfied with not
less than that Christian disciples should be wholly acceptabl
God.

John Wesley, in his Notes on this passage, made an interes
distinction. He wrote: '*Holy*—Toward God. *Spotless*—In yo
selves. *Unreprovable*—As to your neighbour.' Whilst the
distinction may be valuable, it is clear that the Apostle had
mind the divine judgement rather than our neighbour's, a
Corinthians 1^8 makes clear.

This section closes with a plea for perseverance. This let
appears to have been written in part out of a deep concern lest t
converts were led away by false teaching. This concern gives r
to some interesting repetitions in the course of the letter. Here
bids them 'continue in the faith, grounded and steadfast' (ver
23). Later on, he trusts that they will be 'rooted and builded |
in him, and stablished in your faith' (chap. 2^7). This can on
take place if the converts refuse to move away from the hope (
the gospel. Strange doctrines are offered in our day too. Inter
pretations are given to the Scriptures, which are perversions (
New Testament truth, as in the case of Jehovah's Witnesse:
The Christian preacher needs to have a like concern for the com
munity of God's people, ever remembering that the preacher i
'the servant of the gospel' (verse 23).

C. *THE PREACHER'S PRIVILEGE*
(Col. 1^{24}–2^7)

The cost which awaits a true 'servant of the gospel' is now
clearly stated, but also the proud privilege of the one who is permitted to share God's secret with his fellows. In these verses, Paul
describes his aims as a preacher, so that his readers may know
precisely the purposes he has in mind. It is a healthy discipline

period of Paul. For the Apostle, the emphasis lies on the unity that lies in Christ. He does not say, 'bodies', but 'the *body* is one . . . so also is Christ' (II Cor. 12^{12}). In his letter to the Ephesians, he claimed that the Church, as the body, expresses the 'fullness of Christ' (1^{23}), whilst the various ways of service have as their aim to build up the body (4^{12}). Christ's unity with His Church is mirrored in the oneness of marriage (Eph. 4^{30}). Therefore, suffering for the Church meant for Paul suffering with Christ—they belonged eternally together.

1$^{25-29}$. His sphere of work lay particularly among the Gentiles. The Jews were only too conscious of the privileges that belonged to them as the chosen people (Rom. 2$^{17-20}$; 3$^{1-2}$) but the glory of the Christian revelation God's divine secret now disclosed, was that the Gentiles should share in the covenants of promise. This had been hidden from all ages and generations until now—but now God made this known in Christ. Paul was deeply aware of his special responsibility for the Gentiles (Rom. 11^{13}; 15^{16}), which is also expressed here ('to you-ward', verse 25). The work of the preacher is set forth in clear terms. He is (a) to proclaim, to declare the good news from God; (b) to admonish everyone without fear or favour, and (c) to instruct everyone 'in all the ways of wisdom'—all with the sole aim of producing mature Christian disciples.

Certain notes recur in this passage. The message is not just for the Jews but for 'everyone'. There is no limit to its availability, as Paul stresses in his description of the work of the preacher.

2^1. Life has frustrations of all kinds. Here a prisoner, dogged by illness and privations (II Cor. 12^{10}), expresses his concern for those whom he longs to help and yet has never seen. He writes, 'I want you to know how greatly I *agonize* for you and for those at Laodicea.'

2$^{2-7}$. His struggle in prayer is a labour to see the Church truly born in Colosse. The marks of such a Church are clear, namely, encouragement, love, and knowledge. The word he uses for 'comfort' (*parakalein*) may be better expressed as 'spurred on' to a deeper faith, which requires a close-knit love among them. Division and lack of love cause discouragement, whether between individuals or in a community. But for these readers he pleads for unity and knowledge.

It is clear that Paul strives to put down as clearly as possible his intentions for them. He uses three terms for knowledge, bearing in mind the Gnostic background against which the letter is written.

(a) He prays for them to have 'the full assurance of *understanding*', a term which emphasizes the practical application of intellect to action. No one can travel far without taking decisions and choices but these acts of the will should take place with 'the full wealth of conviction' (*NEB*). This may be done if we grasp God's secret in Christ Himself.

(b) This secret enlightens us by a treasury of wisdom (*sophia*) and knowledge (*gnosis*). The term *sophia* refers to man's ability as a rational creature to choose between right and wrong, between truth and error. For the Greek, a man would be a poor creature indeed if he were merely a victim of his passions or the plaything of circumstance. On the contrary, the full-grown adult was expected to take rational choices as a responsible being.

(c) Yet life is not all reason. Some knowledge comes by flashes of insight, by intuition. This is expressed by the term *gnosis*, which has a special significance in this letter.

Gnosis is used to express not only an intuitive grasp of truth but also a term to describe those forms of truth which can only be known by the initiated, by those specially instructed, as with a craft. In this latter sense, it implies an entry into hidden forms of truth, which are known only to the select or the elect. Paul boldly claims that 'all the treasures of hidden gnosis' are in Christ, deliberately using the terms employed constantly by opponents to the Gospel. He adds the further warning, 'Don't be taken in by persuasive speech', which all Christian disciples might well heed in our day and generation.

It is frequently the practice for good people to quote Scriptural terms and passages, filling them with a content of their own. They employ the ancient mould to fashion teaching of their own desiring. The finest safeguard against such practices is to take the teaching and test whether it reveals Christ. If His love and compassion are lacking, then the new pattern is a fraud and the teaching is a lie (I John 4[1-2]). Paul rejoices that this Church has 'order' and 'steadfastness' (firm front: verse 5) as they face their formidable opponents.

This section closes with a plea to examine the foundations of their faith. The Christian needs to walk in Christ, to be rooted in Christ and to be firmly built up in Him. As the sphere of one's life, as soil for strong growth and as foundation of all—Christ alone is sufficient.

D. *FUTILE ALTERNATIVES TO CHRIST*
(Col. 2⁸⁻²³)

How often we wish that we knew more about the background to the teaching of Paul! In the case of these verses, we have mainly to judge the nature of the opposing views by the criticisms which the Apostle directs against them. However, the views are sufficiently clear for us to notice in them certain tendencies which are still present with us in modern times.

Paul expresses his concern that the disciples should stand firm, deeply rooted in Christ, and then proceeds to warn them against attempts to add various practices or doctrines to the adequacy of Christ.

2⁸⁻¹⁰. 'The fullness of Christ' is stressed, as One who is not an ethereal spirit or unearthly demi-god but the One in Whom 'God gives a full and complete expression of Himself' (J. B. Phillips's trans.). The divine nature in the human body of Jesus is unmistakable, so that human beings can share the divine nature (II Peter 1⁴). This emphasis is necessary, as some teachers in Colosse were teaching philosophies which led men away from the simplicity of Christ, 'carrying off (their minds) as a spoil' (as slaves were snatched away by dealers or conquerors). Such elemental philosophies are man-made delusions, empty and vain.

'Elemental' does not mean elementary or simple. In the phrase 'the elemental spirits of the world' this term refers to the belief in powers behind the universe which control human destiny. In particular, it refers to the spirits of the stars and planets, whose activity is the concern of the astrologist. Some newspapers and magazines still today tell their readers what the stars foretell for them. This belief in the influence of the stars is very widespread. It has a very great place in Chinese thought, as it did in Roman and Greek thought. Many great leaders of the past had a firm belief in astrology, as, for example, Alexander the Great and Julius Caesar. Such views are normally deterministic. Man is in the grip of forces, over which he has no control, and by which he is made a mere pawn. However, if a man could secure the influence of some other and greater stellar power, to neutralize or turn aside the bad influence, then such influence was valuable. The astrologist was paid handsomely for charms, amulets, and secret information, to counter the evil influences of planets and stars.

The Gnostic teachers claimed to be able to impart the secret information needed to escape from dangerous destinies, foretold by the stars. Paul believed that the power of Christ was absolutely adequate, as He is in control of 'every power and authority in the universe'. All these other powers, if such they are, are subject to Him.

2^{11-13}. Furthermore, Jewish teachers were among those who wanted to propagate their views or, at any rate, Jewish tendencies were present in these contrary views. The early Church had a stern battle with those who sought to press the requirements of the Jewish Law as essential to the new Gentile Christians (Acts 15^1). The Letter to the Galatians was written to warn Christians against those who wanted to subject the Gospel to the demands of the Jewish Law. For Paul, circumcision (the mark of the true Jew) was a fine practice, if it in fact denoted that the circumcised person was a 'son of Abraham', i.e. that he had the faith of Abraham. Without that righteous faith, the sign was a futile act.

True circumcision was recognized, by Old Testament writers, as the 'outward and visible sign of an inward and spiritual grace'. Thus we find references to uncircumcised lips (Exod. 6^{12}), to the uncircumcised ear (Jer. 6^{10}), and the uncircumcised heart (Lev. 26^{41} and Ezek. $44^{7, 9}$), which were all tokens of disobedience. In contrast was the circumcised heart (Deut. 30^6), which loved the Lord.

As Gentiles, converts to the faith, the Colossians had in any case professed to put away unclean works of the flesh and had given themselves to the Lord. This had taken place in the act of their baptism. As new converts of adult age, the baptism was adult baptism from heathenism into the Christian faith. It was probably by total immersion, when the disciple became one with his Lord in death (to an old life), in passing beneath the water, only to rise to a new life (as he arose out of the water). The symbolism of this act is also stressed in Romans 6^{3-4}.

2^{13-15}. Your old way of life—writes Paul—led to death (Rom. 6^{23}) but God did not leave you in the path that led to spiritual death, even though you were Gentiles. God 'made us alive' with Christ (Eph. 2^5) and in so doing, forgave us those sins which led to death. One is reminded of the valley of dry bones (Ezek. 37^{1-14}), where the Lord quickened dead souls to new life and new hope, when life and hope were gone.

The sins of the past form a debit account against us. They make debts which we can never pay. For the Jew this was clear because the Israelites had accepted the Law with a curse on disobedience (Exod. 24³ and Deut. 27¹⁴⁻²⁶); and this Law he had failed to keep (Rom. 2²¹⁻²⁹). For the Gentile, whilst the law was not a written revelation, yet there was the inner unwritten law of the heart and of the conscience (Rom. 2¹⁴⁻¹⁵). This law had similarly been disobeyed by the Gentile world (Rom. 1²⁸⁻³²). Therefore all men were guilty before God. The charge-sheet of their offences was all too clear, and no man could excuse himself.

Yet God had acted to deal with this parlous situation. Like a scribe who wishes to use his papyrus or vellum again, God had taken the charge-list of men's sins and rubbed them off the list. He had wiped out the record, so that the condemned could begin again. But such an action needed to be made public, to declare the prisoner free. Therefore, as a public notice of acquittal is posted in a prominent place for all to see, so God had 'nailed it to the Cross'. He had executed His judgement in a manner that was unmistakable. Prominent throughout is the initiative of God, even though He had been flouted, disobeyed and dishonoured. Such was His grace, that He wiped out the debt, in full view of men.

It might be argued that the Cross was apparently a defeat for God and for Christ by the principalities and powers which were so much to be feared, and of whom the Gnostics claimed secret knowledge. On the contrary, Paul claims that on the Cross Christ laid aside these cosmic powers as though they were a garment. In fact, He made a public spectacle of His triumph, treating these powers as if they were captives in a procession of triumph! Triumphal processions were great occasions in Paul's time. Paul viewed his work as sharing in Christ's continual triumph over the powers of wickedness (II Cor. 2¹⁴). The powers previously feared are now the captives of the conquering Christ. The same note of triumph is prominent in the hymns of Charles Wesley, for instance in his resurrection hymn (*MHB* 222, verse 1):

> *Our Lord is risen from the dead!*
> *Our Jesus is gone up on high!*
> *The powers of hell are captive led,*
> *Dragged to the portals of the sky. Hallelujah.*

2¹⁶⁻¹⁹. Paul warns his friends against the practices adopted by Gnostic teachers. These included asceticism, the observance of ritual days, a pride in special visions and the worship of angels. Most religions have forms of asceticism, as a means to overcome the demands of the sensual life or to accrue merit. Self-conquest

is essential to spiritual progress (as Paul points out in I Corinthians 9²⁷). But self-discipline may become a rigid asceticism which
inflicts all kinds of suffering on the body, stifling God-given
needs and gifts, with every impulse repressed. This results in
ill-health of body, mind, and spirit. On the other hand, other
Gnostics claimed that the body was evil, and therefore it did not
matter what you did with it. Such a view could justify many
forms of immorality. So all practices must be viewed in the light
of the end: 'the kingdom of God is not eating and drinking but
righteousness and peace and joy in the Holy Spirit' (Rom. 14¹⁷).
Such was his answer.

Similarly, among the Jews and many other peoples, certain
days were specially sacred. Such were the days of the yearly feasts
(Num. 18¹⁸), the Sabbath days (Exod. 20¹⁰), the new moon days
and others. (In the Chinese Calendar, ritual regulations are given
for each day, with a list of permitted duties and of forbidden
ones.) By specially observing these sacred days, men tended to
identify religion with ritual and the former rabbi Paul, who had
entered into a new freedom through Christ, was fearful lest these
new converts might be tied down afresh with new ritualistic
demands.

The claim to special visions needed to be safeguarded with
care. True mysticism may be a gift to a deeply spiritual soul, and
to the Church which nourishes such a soul. But visions and mystical experiences may also lead to conceit and self-delusion.
Therefore the Church is warned, 'Do not allow such people to
rob you of your Christian prize by their claims to special visions'
(verse 18).

Angel-worship had developed from a deepened sense of the
majesty of God. As men realized more intensely the awful holiness of God, so the gulf between men and God yawned more
widely. To bridge the chasm, there developed a belief in various
kinds of intermediaries. For some, this developed into a worship
of these intermediaries. Worship, however, must belong to God
alone, says Paul, and to the beloved Son. Paul clearly states that
such practices are an indication that the believers are not holding
on firmly to the centre of their faith. *Christ* is the Head. The whole
body of the Church is held together and receives its supplies from
Him. Thus only can it grow in accord with God's purpose for it.

2²⁰⁻²³. The practices to which Paul has already referred are no
longer valid for those who are in Christ. The false ways belong
to the 'old life of the flesh', whereas believers in Christ have

buried that life and now live in a 'new and living way'. Ordinances of men, regarding meat and drink, together with false humility and unnatural severity to the body, these are no longer binding for them. They have passed over to a new life, which is not of men but of God.

E. *THE NEW LIFE IN CHRIST*
(Col. 3¹-4¹)

Paul followed in the noble succession of the Old Testament prophets, who linked closely together their doctrine of God and man's duty to his fellows. Religion is closely bound to morality, which expresses in life and practice the reality of a man's faith. Therefore Paul, in several of his letters, states at the beginning his lofty conceptions of the gracious activity of God, and then stresses how there must be a response in us amid the common tasks and duties of our communal life. Thus in Romans, chapters 1-8, we find an account of the work of God, which leads on to the practical human duties outlined in chapters 12-16. Similarly, in the letter to the Ephesians, the theological section closes at chapter 4, verse 16, to be followed in verse 17 with the word '*therefore*' and an outline of the manner of life that issues from such beliefs. So too, Paul's thought in this section of his letter to Colosse is concerned about the out-workings of the great themes already considered.

3¹-⁴. Paul has already referred to the significance of baptism (2¹²), relating it to the experience of dying and rising with Christ. Now he takes up the earlier thread of his thought and bids his readers not merely rise with Christ but set their minds on the eternal things, in which Christ rules. He does not miss the opportunity to remind them of the authority of Christ, in the words 'seated on the right hand of God'. Their standard of values, their judgements on others, their conception of their duties, all need to be viewed not merely from an earthly viewpoint but from a heavenly one. The judgement of men was not the last word, but the judgement of God. This should be their criterion.

Therefore, they should consider themselves dead to the old ways of life. This was not easy, as their former associates lived by the old standards. Some friendships of the old way would have to be given up. Some of the old pleasures would have to be left alone. In fact, the delights and satisfactions of the new way might well be 'hidden' from their friends (i.e. unrecognized). Paul uses the term 'hidden', which was a popular one among Gnostic teachers. They referred to their 'hidden knowledge', so Paul claims that the Christian disciple has his 'hidden treasure' in Christ (cp. *MHB* 108, verse 4).

The close identity of the disciple with his Lord is stressed in the phrase that 'Christ is our life' (verse 4). Paul expressed the same idea very forcibly, at an earlier period, in his letter to the Galatians (2^{20}). Similarly, too, he wrote to the Church in Philippi, 'For to me life is Christ' (1^{21}). This identity is seldom achieved even by most ardent 'lovers of the Cross'. A great musician, artist, or scientist may be said to 'live for his work'. He is totally taken up by his work. This is what Christ meant for the Apostle, whose whole life was dominated by the desire to fulfil the mind of Christ. The purpose of such devotion may not be readily apparent to all; but the Christian's standards and judgements, now hidden from others, will be clear enough when Christ shall appear. He will then cause others to see and He will testify to our loyalty, when we shall share His glory with Him. The hope of Christ's return so often colours Paul's thought as he writes.

3^{5-9a}. The deeds of the old way of life, to which they are now to regard themselves as dead, are only too apparent. These deeds are 'earthy', the practices of the sensual man, whose life is dominated by the things of the flesh. In the ancient world, a new note was struck when the Christians insisted on the virtue of chastity. Sex relationships before marriage and outside marriage were regarded as normal and accepted practice. Virginity was as rare as unwanted children were frequent in such a state of society. Hence the widespread use of abortion and the large numbers of unwanted children left abandoned. So it is that Paul places fornication and uncleanness high up on his list of forbidden practices. Closely linked with them are passion and evil desire, which spring from uncontrolled appetite and unredeemed human nature, especially in the case of passions which bring dishonour (Rom. 1^{26}).

Of the Ten Commandments, only the last—Thou shalt not covet (Exod. 20^{17})—has an inward reference, a concern with inner motive as well as outward practice. This particular command had particular significance for Paul, who found that he could not keep it (Rom. 7^{7-8}). Therefore he had a feeling of guilt, which made him strongly opposed to covetousness, which he calls idolatry (verse 5; cp. Eph. 5^5).

All such practices, whether outward (in the abuse of others) or inward (in the constant desire for more and more) are opposed to the activity of God in His universe. The moral law in the individual life and in the life of society is one. It is the activity of God and it is disastrous when men try to disobey God. The tragedy and sorrow which follows can only be interpreted as 'wrath', yet it is the other face of the love of God. God cannot be rejected with impunity (Gal. 6⁷).

Not only sex relationships but all human contacts need to be controlled and disciplined. Self-centredness, which is idolatry, so often breaks out in action and language, when the individual cannot have his own way. Just as the convert to Christianity took off his old garments before his baptism and put on a new white garment, so it is fitting that our manner of life should have a like change. Paul tells his readers that they should 'take off' the old life and 'put on' the new way, which comes from knowing God in Christ.

The things to be 'taken off' include those expressions of an evil heart to which Jesus referred (Mk 7²⁰⁻²³). Paul here mentions 'anger' (orge—slow-burning, smouldering bad-feeling) and 'wrath' (thumos—sudden gusts of passion), together with 'malice', 'slander' and 'foul language'. Malice (kakia) refers to the vicious mind, which turns all good to evil. 'Slander' (blasphemia) means insulting as well as slanderous speech against one's fellows, which becomes blasphemy when it is directed against God. 'Foul language' and 'lying' are also part of the old life, which now have to be put on one side as no longer of use. The faith ennobles all that it touches. Therefore, human language needs to be redeemed and to be purified to be a suitable channel for the new quality of life. Thus may be seen the fruit of the Spirit (Gal. 5²²⁻²³), in positive contrast to negative out-moded practices.

3⁹ᵇ⁻¹⁴. As the Christian parts with the old life, laying it aside, so there follows the positive action of 'putting on' the new man. In his letter to Rome, Paul wrote that we should walk in 'newness of life' (Rom. 6⁴). This might mean that we live with a new spring in our step and a new joy in our heart, though it refers more particularly to the new quality of our life. The term 'new' is carefully used. The term used here is neos (the recent, the new in reference to time) but the 'new life' is 'being renewed' (anakainow, a term derived from kainos, which means 'new' in terms of quality, such as was unknown before). They had entered into a 'new life', which was not merely fresh and clean but was of an entirely new quality as compared with their earlier experience.

The goal of this 'new life' lay in knowledge (*epignosis*); this was a term beloved of the Gnostics, but here it is knowledge of the Creator's likeness. Here all human divisions and barriers are transcended. The Roman world was united by the Pax Romana, which was enforced by the Imperial government. The spoken Hellenistic lingua franca of the slaves and the merchants also served to bring a measure of unity into the Empire. But great divisions remained—religious, intellectual, and social—which needed some greater power to bring men into unity. In a world like our own, where scientific technology has served to make the whole world a neighbourhood, vast divisions still remain—in economic, social, and political affairs. Yet a potential unity lies at the foundation of all human relationships, the unity which is in our Creator's purpose.

It is this unity which is made clear in the coming of Christ, the 'image of the Creator'. In Him there is no ultimate religious and cultural cleavage—'neither Greek nor Jew'. (In the background lies the bitter shadow of the Maccabaean wars, when Jewry fought to the finish against the domination of Greek religion and culture.) In Him, ceremonial and ritual cleavages were overcome —'neither circumcision nor uncircumcision'. (As the letter to the Galatians shows, the early Church had a hard fight to secure this victory; cp. also Acts 15[1].) In Him, class and cultural barriers were transcended—'neither barbarian nor Scythian'. (To the Greek mind, the outer world of the tribes was one of darkness, other men of crude speech and unlettered minds, worthy only of contempt.) In Him, even the social distinctions were taken away— 'neither slave nor freeman'. (The importance of full citizenship in Greece and Rome was only too well understood. The bondman bore the brunt of the work in a society where slaves outnumbered freemen by three or four to one.) Paul is so emphatic that he states that the barriers 'cannot be . . . in Christ'. Even the apparently fundamental distinction of sex is transcended in the perfect unity of Christ (Gal. 3[28]).

It is clear that the world has still a long way to go, to enter into this conception of Christ's all-embracing oneness. And the divisions between classes and groups are not merely between those in the world but are manifest within the Church. Here too Paul's goal of oneness still lies away ahead of us, in the uncharted sphere of spiritual reality.

To be in Christ is no glib phrase but a fruit-bearing life, manifest in clear paths of conduct. Paul lists the graces to be sought.

How close to his Lord he is! He begins with 'a heart of compassion'—most needful in a hard world. He addresses his words to 'God's elect, holy and beloved', all terms which are used in the Old Testament for Israel but now applied to the Church, the new Israel of God (Gal. 6[16]). There follows a list of the virtues which are the 'expression work' of the new life. These are kindness (*chrestotes*—used of the yoke of Jesus: Matt. 11[30]), humility (a noble recognition of our true state before God), gentleness (the mean between strength and weakness), and longsuffering, which refuses to lose patience with one's fellows. These are the outworkings of the faith, together with the spirit of forgiveness, which is rooted not in our condescension for others, nor in our pride, but in the fact that God has first of all forgiven us. We should treat others as He has treated us, as Jesus taught so clearly in the parable of the unforgiving servant (Matt. 18[21-35]).

Is there any link to bind these qualities together? It is apparent that they are not merely a number of disparate virtues, moral duties for our good, but expressions of the central bond of love. Every community has tendencies to break into cliques unless there is some bond which holds together all groups within it. The 'bond of perfection' (*teleiotes*—maturity) is love, which Paul describes so fully in I Corinthians 13. It is significant that this is the test of full maturity, in social and personal relationships.

3[15-17]. Clad in these new qualities, our discipleship will then be upheld by certain gifts. There is the peace of Christ, which is to act as 'umpire' or 'arbiter' in our hearts. His peace abides with us whilst we keep His rules, but departs when we disobey them. This activity of the peace of Christ is similar to Paul's description in the letter to Philippi (4[7]), in which peace is the 'sentinel' to guard the mind and heart against intruders. To depart from the way of Christ invites division and disorder. To keep in Him brings peace and harmony, which are the evidence of His presence. This peace is not merely individual but communal, indicating that where He is harmony will abide in His body. How far does our Church life bear testimony, by its peace, to His presence? This question might well be asked with regard to wider interchurch relationships. Such peace arises out of our deep sense of gratitude to Him (verse 15).

A further gift is 'the word of Christ', which is able to dwell in the heart. This will provide you with all wisdom. 'The word of Christ' is not a dead verbal idea but is full of potentiality, pregnant with new life, opening up new horizons for the believer.

There is nothing hid from this powerful energy within us (Heb. 4[12-13]). By means of this gift, we are able to teach and advise one another, in ways which naturally rise into song. Praise in Jewish worship found expression in the Psalms of the Temple and Synagogue. Similarly, our praise will find expression in songs—both ancient psalms and modern spiritual songs—in thankfulness for the grace given to us by God. We wish that we possessed more of the hymns composed in the early Church. A fragment of one of them is found in I Timothy 3[16]. Methodism has always taken to heart the advice that a grateful heart should sing. Charles Wesley expressed this need in many of his hymns, as in *MHB* 411 (verse 2a):

> *The name we still acknowledge*
> *That burst our bonds in sunder,*
> *And loudly sing*
> *Our conquering King,*
> *In songs of joy and wonder.*

There follows in this epistle a verse which sums up all that has gone before. Few summaries have stated the Christian Way so simply and lucidly. 'Whatsoever you do, do all in the name of the Lord Jesus' (verse 17). This thought is expressed again in verse 23, as well as in I Corinthians 10[31]. There is one aim—giving thanks (and glory) to God through Him. This echoes the teaching of Jesus in Matthew 5[16].

3[18]-4[1]. Generalities are not enough. Certain groups of people need more specific advice (cp. Lk. 3[10-14]). Perhaps Paul had been asked for such advice. He specifies the particular manner in which Christian wives, husbands, children, fathers, slaves, and masters ought to act to fulfil their calling in the Lord.

It is natural that such advice bears the stamp of contemporary thought. Within Judaism the mother was exalted (Prov. 31[10-31]) but in public life a woman's place was to be submissive, in an essentially patriarchal society. This is apparent in Paul's thought. Yet husbands should love their wives and not be harsh towards them. The attitude towards women rose slowly under the pressure of the Christian ethic, but real partnership between the sexes has been slow in growth.

Towards children the attitude in the pagan world was often harsh. The Roman father had an absolute right to dispose of his children, even to put them to death. Paul upholds the duty of children to honour their parents, but also advises their fathers to avoid hardness, 'lest the children lose heart'. Encouragement is a parental duty. As children grow up, the value for them of the word 'Father' will colour their use of the term 'Our Father', which meant so much to Jesus. If the earthly father is harsh and tyrannical, it will be difficult for the child (even when he has grown to be a man) to use the word 'Father' without revulsion, as Martin Luther found. The discipline of a father needs to be seen to be an expression of love.

Greater attention is given to the Christian behaviour of a slave. A slave had no personal rights. He was not a citizen nor was his master required to treat him as a human being. He was essentially a household tool, which could be laid aside or discarded when age or infirmity rendered him useless. If he lived with a woman (since legal marriage was not possible to a 'thing'), any children born belonged to his master, just as a sheep's lambs belonged to the shepherd.

It is not surprising that many slaves were content to be irresponsible. If they neglected their work, then a harsh master might beat them. If the master was easy-going, they might get away with a minimum of work. There were, no doubt, many slaves in the Church, as I Corinthians 1^{26-29} implies. Paul advises them to be obedient in all things. As Christians, their service was offered to God: 'ye serve the Lord Christ.' Therefore their service must be wholehearted, in singleness of heart. This standard was clearly very high for any servant. Yet Christian service is not for the eyes and approval of men alone but to please the Lord of all (cp. Eph. 6^{5-9}, which states their duty in similar terms). *Free* workmen have an even greater responsibility, as they can *offer* services and work.

On the other hand, the master or employer has his obligations too. He needs to be just and fair. He also has a Master to whom he must give account. God is impartial in His approval of the good.

F. *PRAYER AND FELLOWSHIP*
(Col. 4^{2-18})

As the letter draws to its close, the Apostle gives to his readers his pastoral advice for the Christian way. As the shepherd cares for the flock, so Paul watches over the Gentile converts. He urges the need for constant prayer, wise conduct, and graceful speech. Finally, he commends his friends and sends their greetings to the Church in Colosse. These matters we can now consider in detail.

4^{2-6}. Whenever Paul thinks of his friends at a distance, his thought turns into an act of prayer. In the same way, Richard Baxter thought of those who were in fellowship with Christ yet parted from him in the body:

> *Before Thy throne we daily meet,*
> *As joint petitioners to Thee;*
> *In spirit we each other greet,*
> *And shall again each other see.*
>
> (*MHB* 714, verse 5.)

Such prayer should be constant, with thanksgiving, and should be specific. When Jesus was in the Garden of Gethsemane, that last evening with His disciples, He bid them 'Watch and pray' (Matt. 26^{41}). Paul likewise links together the need to watch and pray. Vigilance is part of the mental equipment of a soldier. It is often difficult, at the close of the day, to keep awake to pray. Christians have to be wakeful (Rom. 13^{11}) as well as prayerful if they are to meet the demands of their situation. Moreover prayer has to be made for perseverance within the Christian fellowship, as Paul points out by his use of the plural ('for us'). This passage has close links in thought and language with his Ephesian letter (6^{18-20}).

In particular, prayer is requested for the Apostle himself. As an 'ambassador in bonds', it took much courage for him to seek to be bolder in his preaching. Prudence would suggest that he took a 'safer' line, that he modulated his zeal, and waited for a more suitable season. Paul's answer to such a suggestion is clear. He asks that they pray at all seasons that he may make known the mystery of the gospel, and—even though he is in chains—that he should speak boldly, as he ought to do (cp. Eph. 6^{20}). In asking their prayers Paul uses the interesting phrase, 'that God may open a door for the word'. It would be of interest to know whether this phrase came often to his mind (cp. I Cor. 16^9). Perhaps Luke heard him use it in his preaching (Acts 14^{27}). It echoes a phrase of Hosea, 'I . . . make the valley of Achor [trouble] a door of hope', though in Paul's usage it simply refers to opportunity, which he was only too ready to grasp. Preaching was not a matter of personal inclination but of intense obligation (I Cor. 9^{16}).

Yet prayer alone is not enough. Wise conduct is part of their witness, as Jesus had told them (Matt. 10^{16}). This must be particularly so in their relationship to others outside the Christian fellowship. Living in two worlds inevitably produced tensions.

Disciples were not to be conformed to the life of the world around them, but must seek to be transformed into the likeness of Christ. Moreover, they had to try to transform that non-Christian world. This is brought home by a vivid phrase from the market-place, 'redeeming the time', which is translated or paraphrased by Dr William Barclay in the phrase, 'Buy up every possible opportunity' (verse 5). Whilst the Christian must be wise, he must not lack zeal in bringing Christ to his fellows, at every opportunity. This phrase may mean, however, 'Make the best use of your time'—a word of advice which John Wesley truly fulfilled in his life and practice. Both the Wesley brothers redeemed the time as evangelists (*MHB* 390, verse 2).

Speech also plays its part in Christian living. Just as meat needs to be seasoned with salt to make it palatable, so speech needs to have winsomeness if it is to provide a suitable reply to our neighbours. Peter gives similar advice to his friends (I Pet. 3[15]). The term used for 'grace' may be translated 'charm' in manner and bearing, which may be heightened by the 'tang' of wit to meet the questions, particularly of opponents. Jesus bids His disciples have salt in themselves (Mk 9[50]), rather than be tasteless and colourless members of society. The tongue may prove to be a good servant but a bad master. Unless it is disciplined, it becomes a veritable means of evil (Jas 3[2-12]). The use of fitting speech may serve as a channel to reach the hidden depths of many a heart.

4[7-18]. The personal qualities of Paul's letters are revealed in the long list of workers from the Church where he is writing the letter, recorded for those in the Church which receives it. The bearers of this epistle are Tychicus and Onesimus. Tychicus also carried the letter to the Ephesians (Eph. 6[21]). This messenger is sent with a double purpose: to tell them about Paul's situation, and to reassure them. Onesimus, who is described as 'a faithful and beloved brother, who is one of you', is no doubt the same person as the former runaway slave—whom Paul returned to his master, with the only surviving letter in the New Testament which is addressed to an individual, namely, the letter to Philemon. Philemon (the master) is not mentioned in the letter to the Colossians but Archippus (4[17]), who was possibly the son of Philemon, is mentioned in both letters.

Paul refers to other helpers, some of whom have special interest as he mentions them elsewhere in other letters. For example, he writes of Aristarchus, who was a Macedonian from Thessalonica

(Acts 20[4]). He was a travelling companion of the Apostle and was seized with Gaius, a fellow-countryman, in the uproar in Ephesus aroused by the silversmiths who profited from the worship of Diana of the Ephesians (Acts 19[29]). This same companion is still at Paul's side, as a fellow-prisoner. Mark also is with Paul, but at liberty. He is described as the cousin of Barnabas, who gave this young John Mark a second chance to redeem himself (Acts 15[36-39]), after Mark had earlier left Paul and Barnabas, on the first missionary journey. By the time this letter was written, Mark had fully won Paul's confidence again; in his last letter Paul longs to have Mark by him (II Tim. 4[11]). Of Justus we know only his name, but he also is described as a comfort to Paul in prison.

Epaphras, to whom reference has already been made (1[7]), remains with Paul, but in his prayers he strives to build up his friends in the Churches in Laodicea and Hireapolis, as well as in Colosse. He has worked hard on behalf of them all. Luke is described as 'the beloved physician', which throws light upon and confirms the evidence of his professional training, his help to the ailing Apostle as well as his marked interest (in his Gospel) in the healing miracles of Jesus. We find him standing by Paul, as in II Timothy 4[10]. The same verse tells us that Demas, after serving with Paul, deserts him—out of love for this present world. In circumstances so testing, friends were sifted out and their true qualities were seen. As Polonius advised his son in *Hamlet*:

> *The friends thou hast, and their adoption tried,*
> *Grapple them to thy soul with hoops of steel.*
>
> (Act I, Sc. 3.)

Then there is Nymphas and the brothers of Laodicea, together with the Church in their house. The simplicity of the early Church is brought out as we are reminded of the Church in the homes of the members. It was not until the 3rd century that a special church building came to be a common practice. It was often in the homes of the Church leaders that the members met. In Jerusalem, the members met in the home of Mary, the mother of John Mark (Acts 12[12]). So in Colosse, the home of Philemon and Apphia served as a meeting place for the Church (Philem. 1-2). This may be the reason for the reference to Archippus (Col. 4[7]), who may have acted as the elder or leader in the Church, meeting in his home. In any case he is encouraged to fulfil his work faithfully.

Paul's letters were no doubt treasured by the Churches, which handed them round in order to pass on news of the Apostle's welfare. Thus there is in verse 16 the instruction that this epistle should be read not only to the Church in Colosse but also to the one in Laodicea. Paul also says that the Laodicean letter should be read in the Church in Colosse. What has happened to this Laodicean letter? It may have been lost. No doubt many of Paul's letters have been lost, in so far as only thirteen of them have survived—and these cover a span of fifteen years. Or this may refer to 'the Letter to the Ephesians', which appears to have been originally a circular letter, not meant for Ephesus alone; and this is the generally-held view today. But again, it could refer to the letter to Philemon.

The letter closes with the signature of the Apostle Paul. He has dictated the letter to a secretary, perhaps Tertius (cp. Rom. 16[22]). There follows the simple reminder, 'Remember my bonds' (cp. Gal. 6[18]), as token of his fidelity to the Gospel and as a stimulus to faith. His final word is of the grace which sustains him, the grace which is for all: 'Grace be with you.'